Selected Topics

LONGMAN
LECTURE
SERIES

Selected Topics

HIGH-INTERMEDIATE
LISTENING
COMPREHENSION

Ellen Kisslinger

Series Editor
Michael Rost

Addison
Wesley
Longman

Selected Topics: High–Intermediate Listening Comprehension

Longman, 10 Bank Street, White Plains, NY 10606

Associated companies:
Longman Group Ltd., London
Longman Cheshire Pty., Melbourne
Longman Paul Pty., Auckland
Copp Clark Pitman, Toronto

Text credits appear on page 145.

Photo credits: Pages 41, 43, 44, and 48 from
TAPESTRIES IN THE SAND by David Villasenor
with permission of Naturegraph Publishers.

Distributed in the United Kingdom by Longman Group
Ltd., Longman House, Burnt Mill, Harlow, Essex CM20
2JE, England, and by associated companies, branches,
and representatives throughout the world.

Acquisitions director: Joanne Dresner
Senior development editor: Debbie Sistino
Production editor: Lisa Hutchins
Text design: The Mazer Corporation
Cover design: Joseph DePinho
Text art: Judy Love, PC&F, Inc.
Production supervisor: Anne Armeny

Library of Congress Cataloging-in-Publication Data

Kisslinger, Ellen.
    Selected topics : intermediate listening comprehension / Ellen
  Kisslinger.
      p.   cm.—(Longman lecture series)
    ISBN 0-8013-0967-0
    1. English language—Textbooks for foreign speakers. 2. English
language—Spoken English. 3. Listening. I. Title. II. Series.
PE1128.K495   1994
428.3'4—dc20   93-21020
                                CIP

11-VG-00

CONTENTS

INTRODUCTION

Selected Topics is an intermediate-level book and audiocassette designed to help English as a second language (ESL) students develop the listening and study skills they need to successfully follow and take notes on academic lectures. The text was carefully developed in response to observations in classrooms of some of the challenges students face as they listen to lectures.

This textbook contains twelve units and twelve recorded lectures, each of which covers a topic that might be offered in a university department. These topics represent a wide variety of disciplines and were selected because of their general appeal to students of varying backgrounds and interests. Students are provided with a stimulating educational experience as they develop the general academic skills they need to do university-level work in their own fields.

The classroom activities focus on the skills students need to succeed, recognizing that there are multiple challenges in an academic situation. Students must be able to understand lectures, take clear and concise notes, and use their notes to either write papers or take tests. With these considerations in mind, this book is designed to:
- develop students' ability to focus on the main ideas of a lecture
- provide students with a good foundation in note-taking skills
- increase students' vocabulary
- develop students' analytical skills
- help students recognize how different types of lectures are organized
- promote speaking ability through cooperative work
- familiarize students with academic test-taking

Each unit has six sections. The activities in the sections are clearly ordered. In order to help you maximize your use of the book, a brief explanation of each section and a suggested procedure for that section is presented. These are only suggestions for using the book successfully.

UNIT ORGANIZATION

Each unit starts with a title and a drawing, map, or other type of visual that introduces the topic of the lecture. By spending a few minutes talking about the title and theme picture, students will begin to think about the topic and begin to predict what might be covered in the lecture. This will help them start to think about what they already know about the topic.

SECTION 1: TOPIC PREVIEW

The **Topic Preview** has two parts: a short reading and a number of questions (Warm-Up Discussion). This section is designed to introduce the topic, to stimulate interest, and to help students think about what they already know about the topic. It will also help them to activate the English vocabulary they already know related to the topic, thus making it more readily available as they listen to the lecture.

Procedure
1. Have students read the paragraph silently. Ask them general comprehension questions such as: What do you think the lecture is going to be about? or What do you know about this topic already?
2. Divide students into pairs or small groups. Give students time to read and discuss the Warm-Up Discussion questions. Call on volunteers to briefly share their ideas with the class. Alternatively, go over the questions as a whole-class discussion activity. This section can be covered in about ten minutes. If there are time constraints, have students look at the questions before class.

SECTION 2: VOCABULARY PREVIEW

The **Vocabulary Preview** contains two parts. The first part is a presentation of ten key words students will hear as they listen to the lecture. The second part is a matching or fill-in-the-blanks exercise using the ten words. The purpose of the vocabulary presentation is to familiarize students with the vocabulary, train them to use context to figure out meaning, and provide them with an opportunity to check their understanding of the meaning. This section takes about ten minutes to complete. It can be assigned in advance as homework.

Procedure
1. Have students read the presentation sentences.
2. Have students complete the matching or fill-in-the-blanks exercise.

3. In pairs, have students compare their answers or check them as a class.

Word Networks contains additional words and expressions in the lecture that may be unfamiliar to the students. It provides a reference for students. It is particularly useful for students for whom the material is challenging and for those who want to develop their vocabulary further. Word Networks can be used either before or after students listen to the lecture.

Procedure

1. Have students read over the word lists. In small groups or as a whole-class activity, talk about the words students have questions about.
2. Check students' understanding by having them create original sentences using some of the words.
3. Encourage students to add to the list any other words from the unit that are new to them.

SECTION 3: LISTENING TO THE LECTURE

The lectures have been recorded on audiocassette. They have been recorded twice. Each lecture is divided into two sections. The first recording includes a narrator who introduces each section, gives students a brief preview of what each section is about, and provides some clues about the lecture's organization. The second recording has no narrator.

Section 3 includes a prelistening focus question and two sets of comprehension questions. The first set of questions checks general understanding of the main ideas. The second set checks understanding of additional facts and details that support the main ideas. It is important to spend ample class time on this section. About fifteen minutes is recommended for most classes.

Procedure

BEFORE YOU LISTEN

1. Read the prelistening focus question aloud or have the students read it. Emphasize that there is no single correct answer here.
2. Ask volunteers for their answers.

FIRST LISTENING: MAIN IDEAS

1. Ask students to quickly read the questions in order to focus their listening.
2. Play the lecture. Stop the tape after each section to allow students to quickly answer the questions.

3. Have students compare their answers in pairs or as a class.

SECOND LISTENING: FACTS AND DETAILS

1. Follow the same procedure as for First Listening. Either rewind the tape or continue with the second recording of the lecture, which has no narrator.
2. Check the answers. The answers are provided in **Appendix B**.

SECTION 4: TAKING NOTES

Section 4 consists of an instruction box with note-taking advice and a model for taking notes based on the technique or strategy presented. This section helps students approach note taking in an organized way. One goal is to familiarize students with a variety of note-taking techniques and to help them find techniques that work well for their individual styles of learning. The model helps the students see clearly how the technique can be used.

Procedure

1. Have students read the instruction box at the top of the page.
2. On the board, give an example of the technique or note-taking strategy presented.
3. Play the lecture again as students take notes using the model given.
4. In pairs, have students compare their notes. Encourage students to help each other correct their notes and resolve inconsistencies. It is important to allow students ample time to go over their notes together. It is an excellent opportunity not only to improve their speaking skills, but to boost their self-confidence in their listening skills.

SECTION 5: REVIEWING THE CONTENT

In this section, the students review their notes and discuss with their classmates in a structured way the content of the lecture. These activities provide them with an opportunity to make sure they have an overall grasp of the content of the lecture. This section consists of the following parts: an instruction box that contains a strategy for reviewing the lecture; **Using Your Notes,** in which students use the strategy presented in the instruction box; **Preparing for the**

Test, in which students answer questions on the vocabulary and general content of the lecture; **Review: Final Listening,** in which students listen to the lecture a final time; and **Taking the Test,** in which students complete a Review Test.

The Review Test contains two parts. Part I checks understanding of some of the key vocabulary of the unit in either a multiple-choice or fill-in-the-blanks format. A word box of appropriate words and expressions from which students can select their answers is included in the fill-in-the-blanks format. Part II checks understanding of the main ideas in the lectures. It contains two short-answer exam questions, each followed by a short cloze paragraph that becomes a sample answer to the question. Students are asked to complete each cloze paragraph using words from the word box. There are fifteen items in each Review Test. The Review Tests are provided in **Appendix A.**

The Review Test gives teachers a way to evaluate students' understanding of the lecture material. It gives students an opportunity to see what they have learned and to practice test–taking. The cloze paragraph format gives students an opportunity to become familiar with how to answer a short-answer exam question without having to generate the complete answer themselves. Many students do not have experience in answering short-answer questions. This can be a serious problem for them in their university work. At this level of proficiency, it seems both useful and appropriate to provide students with a model for how an answer should be formulated.

Procedure

1. Have students read the instruction box. Give them an example of how to review their notes using the technique presented. Ask students to give additional examples if the technique still seems unclear.
2. **Using Your Notes.** Give students time to complete the activity. As a class, check the students' work.
3. **Preparing for the Test.** In pairs, have students answer the questions. Circulate and answer any questions they may have.
4. **Review: Final Listening.** Play the tape a final time. Encourage students to ask questions.
5. **Taking the Test.** Have students turn to the Review Test.

Part I: Have students complete the answers.
Part II: For each question, have the students
- read the question. Make sure they understand what the question is asking them to do.
- read over the entire cloze paragraph to get an idea of how the paragraph is organized and what it says.
- reread and fill in the blanks using the word box provided.
- read through the completed paragraph.

To check their answers, have students turn to the Answer Key in **Appendix B** or call on students to read the paragraphs for the class.

Giving the Review Test in the next class after the presentation of the lecture helps train students to recall information. Decide whether or not to time the Review Test. Timing it will make it more like an academic testing situation. Decide whether or not to let students use their notes during the Review Test. This is a pedagogical decision based on the emphasis of the class. If the emphasis is on learning to take good notes that can be drawn on later, allowing the use of the notes during the Review Test is consistent with this goal. If the emphasis of the class is on simulating an academic situation in which recalling information at exam time is valued, then not allowing students to use their notes is consistent with this goal.

SECTION 6: EXPANSION

This section contains a creative and challenging activity that is thematically related to the topic of the lecture. The activities and procedures vary from lesson to lesson. Some of the units contain information gap activities in which students must share information in order to complete the task. Although the emphasis is primarily on developing speaking and listening skills, many of these activities can be supplemented with writing activities and library work.

THE LECTURES

The recorded lectures are intended to simulate the experience of listening to an actual academic lecture. At this stage of proficiency, students benefit from lectures that have some redundancy, some recycling of ideas. The lectures were recorded to sound as authentic as possible and include hesitations, false starts, and pauses.

The Lecture Scripts

The transcript for each lecture is provided in the back of the book in **Appendix C**. The transcript can be used to prepare for presentation of the lecture. It can also be used by the students after the unit has been completed. Students should be discouraged from looking at the transcript until after the Review Test. It is always important to keep in mind that the primary goal of the book is to help the students develop their listening and note-taking skills. If student use of the transcripts becomes a problem, they can be removed from the students' books.

A FINAL COMMENT TO THE STUDENT

The goal of this book is to help you develop the skills you need to successfully follow, take notes on, and use the information you hear in academic lectures. It takes a lot of practice to be able to pay attention and listen for a long time. Having good note-taking skills will make it easier for you to follow the lectures you have to listen to. As you use this book, think about developing a style of taking notes that works for you.

There are a variety of topics in this book. It offers opportunities for you to think about topics that you may or may not be familiar with. Enjoy using this book as you develop the skills you need to succeed.

ACKNOWLEDGMENTS

A number of people helped with this book. I greatly appreciate the suggestions and comments of my colleagues, in particular, Jennifer Bixby, Ann Gleason, Elly Schottman, and Ruth and Mensah Adjogah. My family contributed content as well as moral support through the process. The reviewers—Steve Thewlis, Joseph McVeigh, Sandra Soghikian, David Beglar, Neil Murray, Linda Schlam, Helen Solorzano, Laurie Fazier, and Malcolm Benson—provided invaluable comments and suggestions on earlier versions of the book. The support and direction provided by the many people at Longman brought the book to fruition. Lastly, I'd like to thank Michael Rost, my long-time friend, without whom this book would never have happened. His planning and development of the series, as well as his advice and unflagging support, made this book possible.

LONGMAN
LECTURE
SERIES

Selected Topics

A GOOD MANAGER

1 TOPIC PREVIEW

If we look in a dictionary it will say "A manager is the person in charge. The person who directs, controls, and handles a business or organization." When we think about our dream job, the job we would love to have, it often includes being the manager, or having a good manager. The management style of the person in charge is very important. What makes someone a good manager?

WARM-UP DISCUSSION

In pairs or small groups, discuss these topics with your classmates.

1. What is a good manager like?
2. What is a bad manager like?
3. Have you had a work experience in which the manager was especially good or bad? What happened?

2 VOCABULARY PREVIEW

Read the following sentences and try to guess the meaning of the words in *italics*.

1. The weather would ***vary*** all day; it would change from warm one minute to cool the next.
2. She has a good work ***style***. She is organized, neat, and fast.
3. The boy had a bad ***attitude*** about school; he thought it was a waste of time.
4. The new students were ***enthusiastic*** about school. They liked it a lot.
5. The man was ***content*** at work. He was satisfied with his job.
6. People who work together are ***coworkers***.
7. The company has a very large ***staff***. Over 500 people work there.
8. The office ***manager*** has a responsible job. He needs to make sure everyone does a good job.
9. The manager tried a new system, then ***assessed*** the results. He checked to see what worked well and what didn't work well.
10. People need to sleep. Like air and water, sleep is ***essential*** for us.

Now fill in the blanks in the sentences below. Use the correct form of the words from above.

1. The employee had a bad _____attitude_____. She complained a lot.

2. The meeting was _____. We needed to find out what to do.

3. The family didn't like to travel. They were _____ to stay home and rest on their vacation.

4. His poor work _____ caused many problems in the office.

5. The _____ at the bank are all hard-working people.

6. After making some changes, we met to _____ the results.

7. The teacher _____ the lesson from day to day. She never did the same thing two days in a row.

8. The _____ planned a meeting for Tuesday afternoon. She wanted to discuss a problem in the office.

9. Bonnie and four of her _____ went to the park for lunch.

10. The staff was _____ about the new project. Everyone liked it.

WORD NETWORKS

These are some other words you will hear in the lecture. Read the list. Ask about and discuss any words you do not know.

Actions
organized
run (an office)
complain
focuses
expected
communicating

People and things
situation
technique
employee
opportunity
truth
consultants
assessment
relationship
decisions

Other
irritated
personal
honestly

3 LISTENING TO THE LECTURE

BEFORE YOU LISTEN

You are going to listen to a lecture about being a manager. What do you think makes a good manager? Write three words or phrases that describe a good manager.

1. _____

2. _____

3. _____

FIRST LISTENING: MAIN IDEAS

Listen to each part of the lecture to find out the main ideas. Circle a, b, or c.

PART 1

1. Linda talked to Mr. Thomas because
   a. she was interested in getting a new job.
   b. she was having problems doing her job.
   c. she wanted to have an easier job.

2. Mr. Thomas decided to talk with his staff because he realized
   a. he was angry with Linda.
   b. he didn't want to hear them complain.
   c. other employees might feel the same way as Linda.

PART 2

1. To assess a manager means to point out his or her
   a. good points.
   b. bad points.
   c. good and bad points.

2. Good assessment questions must be
   a. direct kinds of questions.
   b. easy to answer honestly.
   c. easy to listen to.

Employee: _____   Date: _____
Name of Manager: _____
Company Office: _____

1.   Do I give clear directions?

2.   Do you need help from coworkers to understand what I want?

3.   Do I change my mind too often about what I want you to do?

4.   Do I listen to new ideas and ways of doing things?

5.   Do you come to me when you need help?

6.   Do I tell you when you have done a good job?

SECOND LISTENING: FACTS AND DETAILS

Listen to each part of the lecture again. This time listen to learn more facts and details. Answer the questions below. Write T (true) or F (false) in front of each sentence.

PART 1

1. _____ Linda felt she was causing the problems.

2. _____ At first Mr. Thomas was glad Linda came to see him.

3. _____ Mr. Thomas didn't think teamwork was important.

4. _____ According to the speaker, a good manager must let employees talk.

PART 2

1. _____ The best way to ask assessment questions is at an office meeting.

2. _____ The manager should first give the questions in writing.

3. _____ A question like "How would it be easier to do your job?" focuses on the work to be done, not just the manager.

4. _____ According to the lecture, management assessment is a good way to build teamwork.

4 TAKING NOTES

GETTING STARTED TAKING NOTES

To be a good listener, you need to have good note-taking techniques. You must be able to write down the important ideas quickly. If you try to write down every word the speaker says, you will be left behind. A speaker often tells you at the beginning of a lecture how the lecture will be organized. A good habit is to listen *very carefully* to the introduction. This will help you concentrate on what the important ideas of the lecture are. It will help you prepare to take notes.

In the introduction of this lecture, the speaker says: Now *first*, I'll describe a work situation for you . . . and *then* I'll explain one important management technique." This tells you what to listen for.

LISTEN AGAIN

Listen to the lecture again. This time take notes using the model shown below. Add to the information given. Compare your notes with a classmate's.

```
Work Situation
Linda's problem
   —difficulty doing her work
   —office was organized differently
How Mr. Jones felt
   —surprised
   —irritated
Management Technique
Management assessment
   —what it is: tell a manager his or her good and bad
     points
   —how it is done:
Management assessment form
   —how to use it: have employees write their answers
   —type of questions:
Conclusion
   —management styles: vary from culture to culture
   —teamwork is important
```

REVIEWING THE CONTENT

WRITING DEFINITIONS

This lecture gives you some general information about being a good manager. It describes one management technique a good manager can use. One way to remember the information is to try to say it in your own words. For example, you might say:

A good manager *understands that a good staff is important.*

A good manager *knows the employees need to work as a team.*

A good manager *helps people feel that what they do is important.*

If you make a list of statements like these, together they will define what a good manager is and does.

USING YOUR NOTES

Look at the lecture notes you have just written. On a piece of paper make a list of statements about what a good manager is and does. Use your own words. Compare your statements with a classmate's.

PREPARING FOR THE TEST

In your next class, you will take a short test on the lecture. Before the test, be sure to review the following questions. Use your notes as you review.

1. Do you know the meaning of the following words?
   a. staff   **c.** coworkers   **e.** assess   **g.** style   **i.** vary
   b. enthusiastic **d.** essential   **f.** attitude   **h.** content **j.** manager
2. Why did Linda talk to Mr. Thomas?
3. Why did Mr. Thomas decide to talk to Linda's coworkers?
4. What is management assessment?
5. What is one way to do management assessment?

REVIEW: FINAL LISTENING

Now listen one last time to the lecture. Follow your notes as you listen. If you still have any questions, ask your teacher.

TAKING THE TEST

If you have reviewed the material, you should be ready to take the Review Test. Turn to page 97 and answer the questions.

EXPANSION

Read the paragraphs and chart below. When you look at the chart, decide which statements apply to U.S. culture and which apply to your own culture. Then compare your answers in small groups.

The company described in the lecture was a U.S. company. When Linda went to talk to the manager, she believed that the manager would understand her problems because they had the same general way of looking at the world. She seemed to be correct. She was able to communicate to him what was wrong. But what if he wasn't from the same culture? The communication may not have been as smooth.

The culture that people come from affects how they work, how they manage, and how they expect other people to work. In an international company, communication may not go well if the people don't understand how their different cultures affect the way they do business.

Cultural values

1. You can change something you do not like.
2. You must work hard to succeed.
3. An employee must think of the company first.
4. Family and friends are more important than the company.
5. An employee should try to get a better job with higher pay.
6. An employee has a job for life.
7. It is OK to have your own opinions and ideas.
8. Competition makes people work harder.
9. Managers can make important decisions without talking to others.
10. Managers can learn from the staff.

Answer these questions in small groups or as a whole class.

1. What do you think would make someone a good manager in an international business?
2. Would the management assessment presented in the lecture work in your own country? Explain.

COMPUTERS AND HOW WE TALK

LUNCH SPECIALS
- Seafood Salad and corn soup
- Lasagna and garden salad
- Bean soup with bread and cheese
  choice of drink

INTERFACE YOUR APPETITE WITH OUR
DELICIOUS LUNCH SPECIALS!

1 TOPIC PREVIEW

Computers are everywhere in our lives. At grocery stores, banks, schools, hospitals, and factories, everyone is using computers. We know that computers have changed our lives. Have computers also changed the way we talk? Along with the spread of computers, the use of computer words has increased. It's interesting to look at the way computer words are being used in daily life.

WARM-UP DISCUSSION

In pairs or small groups, discuss these topics with your classmates.

1. What have you done so far today? For which things were computers used in some way? Make a list.
2. What computer words or expressions do you know in English?
3. In your own language are any computer words or expressions used in daily life?

VOCABULARY PREVIEW

Read the following sentences and try to guess the meaning of the words in *italics*.

1. I go for a walk *daily.* I walk to the park every day at 7:00 P.M.
2. The boy made ten *errors* in his homework. He had to correct those mistakes.
3. The older brother *influenced* his younger brother in many ways. The younger brother seemed to like everything his brother liked.
4. Changing jobs had a big *impact* on my life. Everything seemed to change.
5. I'll be *available* after 4:00 P.M. I'll have time to see you then.
6. The water *reflected* the boat. It seemed like there were two boats, not one, in the lake.
7. I have a busy *schedule* today. First I have a meeting, then lunch, then two more meetings in the afternoon.
8. Please don't speak medical *jargon* to me. I'm not a doctor. Just tell me in simple words what is wrong with my back.
9. Should I call you at a *particular* time, or is any time all right?
10. My brother had a hard time making the *transition* from being a student to working full-time for a bank. The change was difficult for him to adjust to.

Now match each word with its correct definition.

1. ___*g*___ daily
2. _____ errors
3. _____ influenced
4. _____ impact
5. _____ available
6. _____ reflected
7. _____ schedule
8. _____ jargon
9. _____ particular
10. _____ transition

a. a plan of activities
b. specific; certain
c. a word only used by a special group
d. mistakes
e. the process of making a change
f. affected a person or thing
g. every day
h. showed as through a mirror
i. not busy or in use
j. an effect or impression

WORD NETWORKS

These are some other words and phrases you will hear in the lecture. Read the list. Ask about and discuss any words or phrases you do not know.

Actions
allow
continue
disconnect
suppose

People and things: General words
bank accounts
hairstyles
project
mirror
society

People and things: Computer words
system
software
program

Other
directly
long-term

3 LISTENING TO THE LECTURE

BEFORE YOU LISTEN

You are going to hear a lecture about how computers are changing the way we talk. If someone says, "Your plan has some bugs in it," what do you think he or she means?

FIRST LISTENING: MAIN IDEAS

Listen to each part of the lecture to find out the main ideas. Circle a, b, or c.

> *OFFICE MEMO*
>
> *To all employees:*
>
> *There will be no memo-writing class today. We have decided to take the class off-line this month. A new class will begin the first Thursday of next month. More information will be given later. Thank you.*

PART 1

1. The speaker's main point is that
   a. you can now use a computer to learn a language.
   b. the use of computers and the use of computer words have both increased.
   c. computers have completely changed the words we use in our daily lives.

2. The four examples given support the main idea that
   a. a computer can tell us which clothes to buy.
   b. computers can be used to choose hairstyles.
   c. computer words have spread into daily use.

PART 2

1. The word *bug* is an example of a
   a. word only used by computer people.
   b. word the speaker thinks will be forgotten.
   c. computer word that may become part of the language.

2. The speaker uses the phrase "Language is a mirror of society" to mean
   a. language shows us how our society is changing.
   b. language shows us what is wrong with society.
   c. computers will always influence how we talk.

"I just can't access where I put my keys."

SECOND LISTENING: FACTS AND DETAILS

Listen to each part of the lecture again. This time listen to learn more facts and details. Answer the questions below. Write T (true) or F (false) in front of each sentence.

PART 1

1. _____ The speaker believes we shouldn't do anything without computers.

2. _____ If a company decides to put a project on-line, they don't want to work on it any longer.

3. _____ If I try to interface my schedule with yours, I can't remember what your schedule is.

4. _____ If I can't access where my keys are, I forgot where I put them.

PART 2

1. _____ To get with the program means to do what you're supposed to do.

2. _____ A word that starts out as jargon may gradually be used by many people in daily conversation.

3. _____ A plan with a lot of bugs will probably be successful.

4. _____ The speaker says computers are a mirror of our society.

TAKING NOTES

USING COLUMNS TO ORGANIZE YOUR NOTES

Good notes must be well organized. They need to make important information easy to remember. They also need to be short and clear. Your goal is to have as little to read as possible when you need to review the lecture.

A good way to take notes is to:

Divide your paper into two columns. Make the left column $\frac{1}{3}$ of the page, the right column $\frac{2}{3}$ of the page. In the right column, write your notes. In the left column, write words to help you remember how the lecture was organized.

At the end of the introduction of this lecture, the speaker says, " . . . let me give you some examples from English." This is an important signal to you that some examples will be given. The speaker then continues, "The first example is . . . ," "The second example is . . . ," and so on.

This helps you focus on how the lecture will be organized. You can take notes in the right column and label the examples in the left column.

LISTEN AGAIN

Listen to the lecture again. Before you begin, divide your paper into two columns. Take notes in the right column. Write *Introduction,* then *Example 1, Example 2,* and so on in the left column as shown below. Compare your notes with a classmate's.

Introduction:	Computers have changed our lives. Computers have changed the words we use.
Example 1:	On-line. Have the project on-line. Started or working. Have project going.
Example 2:	Off-line. Take the discussion off-line. Disconnect, take out. Stop talking for now.

REVIEWING THE CONTENT

REREADING YOUR NOTES

It is important to get in the habit of reading your notes after a lecture. This will help you remember the lecture and fix the information in your mind. For each example in this lecture, you are given four pieces of information. As you review your notes, you should have the following for each example:

1. The number of the example
2. The word or phrase
3. What it means in daily life
4. What it means in computer talk

You can mark your notes to highlight these. For example, you can write *DL* to mark what an expression means in daily life. You can write *C* to mark what it means for computers.

This is shown for Example 1.

Example 1 on-line
　　　　　working, part of the system C
　　　　　started, going DL

USING YOUR NOTES

Look at the lecture notes you have just written. As you reread your notes, mark your notes *DL* and *C* to highlight the information. Compare your notes with a classmate's.

PREPARING FOR THE TEST

In your next class, you will take a short test on the lecture. Before the test, be sure to review the following questions. Use your notes as you review.

1. Do you know the meaning of the following words?
   a. daily　　**c.** errors　　**e.** influenced　**g.** impact　　**i.** reflected
   b. particular　**d.** schedule　**f.** jargon　　**h.** available　**j.** transition
2. According to the speaker, what is the relationship between computers and how we talk?
3. What are some examples given in the lecture?
4. What is the word *bug* an example of?
5. What does the expression "Language is a mirror of society" mean here?

REVIEW: FINAL LISTENING

Now listen one last time to the lecture. Follow your notes as you listen. If you still have any questions about the lecture, ask your teacher.

TAKING THE TEST

If you have reviewed the material, you should be ready to take the Review Test. Turn to page 99 and answer the questions.

EXPANSION

Look at the cartoons below. Read the Word Key then fill in the blanks.
Compare your answers with a classmate's.

ROM OR HIGH RES?

WORD KEY

ROM   A read-only-memory, a ROM, is a
computer part. It is a memory unit,
containing information permanently
stored when the unit is manufactured. It
cannot be changed by the person using
the computer. If someone is a read-only-
memory, he or she never learns anything.

HIGH RESOLUTION   A computer
screen that has high resolution is a
computer screen that is clear; it has
good, sharp images. If I say to you, "My
sister, she's high res," what do you think
this means? It means she is intelligent,
clever, and quick, not dull or boring.

Work with a partner. Use an example from the lecture and draw a
cartoon like the ones above. Show your cartoon to another pair and see
if they can guess which example it is about.

BE CAREFUL: PHOBIAS

"This isn't the right job for me!"

1 TOPIC PREVIEW

Most people are afraid of something. Some people are afraid of the dark. Others are afraid of cats or of driving on busy streets. There are some people who do not just have a normal fear of something; they have a phobia. A phobia is different from just being afraid. A phobia is an extreme fear. It is a very strong reaction to something. *Phobia* comes from the Greek word *phobos,* which means fear. Phobias are named by using the Latin or Greek word for the thing feared, and adding the word *phobia.* For example, *areophobia* means fear of flying; *zoophobia* means fear of animals. What do you think *electrophobia* means?

WARM-UP DISCUSSION

In pairs or small groups, discuss these topics with your classmates.

1. What are three common things people are afraid of? Make a list.
2. What are you afraid of? What are people in your family afraid of?
3. Someone who has acrophobia doesn't like ladders, towers, and tall buildings. What do you think acrophobia is?

VOCABULARY PREVIEW

Read the following sentences and try to guess the meaning of the words in *italics*.

1. The weather is ***extreme;*** it is either very hot or very cold.
2. The scientist had a new ***theory.*** To test his idea, he needed to do some experiments.
3. The car accident ***caused*** the woman to have a bad back.
4. Two ***symptoms*** of a cold are a runny nose and sneezing.
5. The woman ***reacted*** to the sad news by laughing. Her response surprised people.
6. The doctor gave me medicine to ***treat*** my cold. I felt much better the next day.
7. The woman had two ***characteristics*** that helped me remember her: a wonderful laugh and big, dark blue eyes.
8. The boy had a little cough. It ***developed*** overnight into a bad cold.
9. I usually wake up at 7:00 A.M. and go to bed at 11:00 P.M. That is my ***normal*** schedule.
10. The gardener ***classified*** the plants into two groups: plants that need a lot of sun and plants that need little sun.

Now match each word with its correct definition.

1. ___c___ theory
2. _____ normal
3. _____ characteristics
4. _____ caused
5. _____ treat
6. _____ reacted
7. _____ classified
8. _____ extreme
9. _____ symptoms
10. _____ developed

a. features
b. made something happen
c. an idea that explains something
d. put into groups
e. very strong; severe
f. signs that something is not normal
g. responded
h. regular; usual
i. became
j. take care of

WORD NETWORKS

These are some other words you will hear in the lecture. Read the list. Ask about and discuss any words you do not know.

Actions
continues
control
imagine

People and things
psychologists
experience
goal

Other
reasonable
Greek
Latin
emotional
strict

3 LISTENING TO THE LECTURE

BEFORE YOU LISTEN

You are going to hear a lecture about what a phobia is and two theories about why people have phobias. Why do you think people have phobias?

_____

FIRST LISTENING: MAIN IDEAS

Listen to each part of the lecture to find out the main ideas. Circle a, b, or c.

PART 1

1. According to the lecture, there are _____ characteristics of a phobia.
   a. two
   b. four
   c. three

2. To write the name of a phobia, first write _____, then *phobia*.
   a. the thing that is feared
   b. fear of water
   c. fear of sleep

PART 2

1. One theory is that a phobia is
   something
   a. we control.
   b. we learn.
   c. we imagine.

2. Another theory is that a phobia is
   a. a sign of a deeper problem.
   b. a deeper problem.
   c. a problem we can't treat.

SECOND LISTENING: FACTS AND DETAILS

Listen to each part of the lecture again. This time listen to learn more facts and details. Answer the questions below. Write T (true) or F (false) in front of each sentence.

PART 1

1. _____ A phobia is a very strong reaction.

2. _____ A phobia isn't difficult to control.

3. _____ Hypnophobia is a fear of water.

4. _____ Phonophobia is a fear of talking on the telephone.

PART 2

1. _____ A child may develop cynophobia from a dog bite.

2. _____ Cynophobia cannot be learned from someone else.

3. _____ A phobia may be a sign of a deeper emotional problem.

4. _____ People cannot learn to control their phobias.

4 TAKING NOTES

FOCUSING ON KEY WORDS

During a lecture, you may notice that certain words or phrases are stressed and repeated. You hear them again and again in the lecture. These words are often called *key words*. They are words that you need to understand to have a general idea of what the lecture is about.

LISTEN AGAIN

Listen to the lecture again. This time pay attention to these words and phrases:

phobia	three characteristics	Greek or Latin names	hydro
cyno	phono	one theory	the other theory
how the phobia is treated			

In your notes, give a short definition or explanation of each one as shown in the example below. Compare your notes with a classmate's.

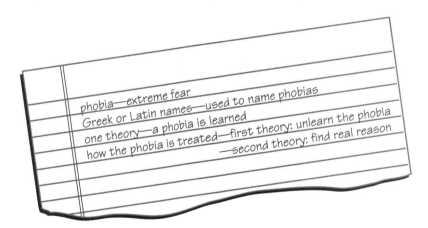

phobia—extreme fear
Greek or Latin names—used to name phobias
one theory—a phobia is learned
how the phobia is treated—first theory: unlearn the phobia
—second theory: find real reason

REVIEWING THE CONTENT

REMEMBERING THE LECTURE USING KEY WORDS

In this lecture you heard some key words. You need to know these words to understand the lecture. In your notes you wrote down these key words to help you remember what you heard. Now you can read over your notes and look for these key words and phrases. Do you know what they mean? Do you understand the main ideas of the lecture?

USING YOUR NOTES

Look at the lecture notes you have just written. Look at each key word or phrase and the description you wrote. Discuss them with a partner. Together decide what five important ideas of the lecture are.

PREPARING FOR THE TEST

In your next class, you will take a short test on the lecture. Before the test, be sure to review the following questions. Use your notes as you review.

1. Do you know the meaning of the following words?
   a. classified **c.** treat **e.** developed **g.** theory **i.** caused
   b. reacted **d.** normal **f.** symptoms **h.** extreme **j.** characteristics
2. What is a phobia?
3. What are the three characteristics of a phobia?
4. How are phobias classified? List at least two examples.
5. What are the two theories about why people have phobias?

REVIEW: FINAL LISTENING

Now listen one last time to the lecture. Follow your notes as you listen. If you still have any questions about the lecture, ask your teacher.

TAKING THE TEST

If you have reviewed the material, you should be ready to take the Review Test. Turn to page 101 and answer the questions.

6 EXPANSION

The paragraphs below describe two more phobias. Work with a partner. Decide who will read which paragraph. Cover the one you do not read. Then take turns explaining what you read and do the activities that follow.

Claustrophobia is the fear of being in closed spaces. People who have claustrophobia become very uncomfortable in an elevator, an airplane, or a small room. They feel like there isn't enough air; that they cannot breathe. On a Sunday, a person with claustrophobia would most likely prefer mountain climbing to going to a movie theater.

People with agoraphobia are afraid of places where there are a lot of people. It is very difficult for them to be in public places such as theaters, trains, buses, stores, banks, or restaurants—any place where there are many people. Most people with agoraphobia don't want to leave home. They are afraid to go outside. Agoraphobia can be a very big problem. It is difficult to live a normal life if you have agoraphobia.

Decide if each job would be bad for someone who had claustrophobia or agoraphobia:

grocery store clerk	forest ranger	public park attendant
submarine operator	zookeeper	
elevator operator	coal miner	

Now take turns asking and answering questions about the phobias discussed in the lecture. First look at the example below.

A: My son washes his hands all the time. What do you think is wrong with him?
B: Maybe he has mikrophobia.

NOTE: Mikrophobia is a fear of germs.

A LESSON IN FOLKTALES

1 TOPIC PREVIEW

Each culture has its own folktales. The Effendi Nasreddin is a Muslim folk hero. He is known throughout North Africa, the Middle East, and Central Asia. He is very popular in China. There are hundreds of Effendi Nasreddin stories. In the stories, the Effendi is a worker, a common man. He is intelligent, clever, and a rebel. He likes to fight back against people who are rich and powerful. He shows us how poor, common people are often wise and how rich people in power can be very foolish.

WARM-UP DISCUSSION

In pairs or small groups, discuss these topics with your classmates.

1. Do you know any folk heroes like the Effendi?
2. What are the names of some folktales from your culture?
3. Do you have a favorite folktale? What is it?

VOCABULARY PREVIEW

Read the following sentences and try to guess the meaning of the words in *italics*.

1. The man had to go to ***court*** because he stole a car. At the court, he found out what would happen to him.
2. The ***judge*** decided that the man would go to jail for two years.
3. The father ***punished*** his daughter for stealing some candy from a store. She had to go to bed early for one week.
4. The mother became ***upset*** when her son broke a window. She started yelling.
5. I have an ***elder*** brother. He is five years older than I am.
6. The man made a ***foolish*** mistake. He should have been more careful.
7. The man didn't have much money, only a few small ***coins.***
8. We put bells on the door. The bells ***jingle*** when someone opens the door.
9. The boy couldn't ***solve*** the math problems. He just couldn't answer them no matter how hard he tried.
10. The family had many ***debts.*** They owed everyone money.

Now match the words with their correct definitions.

1. ___h___ coins
2. _____ court
3. _____ jingle
4. _____ punished
5. _____ judge
6. _____ upset
7. _____ elder
8. _____ debts
9. _____ solve
10. _____ foolish

a. things you owe someone
b. made someone pay for a wrong action
c. the person in court who makes decisions
d. get an answer for; figure out
e. older
f. silly; unwise
g. unhappy; angry
h. small, metal money
i. the place where judges make decisions
j. make a sound like bells

WORD NETWORKS

These are some other words and phrases you will hear in the lecture. Read the list. Ask about and discuss any words or phrases you do not know.

Actions
belonged to
saved

People and things
belt
copper
common people

Other
unfair
ill
impatiently
powerful
stupid
immoral
wise

3 LISTENING TO THE LECTURE

BEFORE YOU LISTEN

You are going to hear a story called "A Dinner of Smells." Look at the title again. What do you think a dinner of smells is?

_____

FIRST LISTENING: MAIN IDEAS

Listen to each part of the lecture to find out the main ideas. Circle a, b, or c.

PART 1

1. Why did the man visit the Effendi?
   a. He was rich.
   b. He had a problem.
   c. He went to court.

2. The restaurant owner wanted money because the man
   a. took some food.
   b. ate some food.
   c. smelled some food.

PART 2

1. The judge decided the poor man
   a. had to pay some money.
   b. didn't do anything wrong.
   c. shouldn't have eaten the food.

2. Who uses power unfairly here?
   a. The Effendi.
   b. The restaurant owner.
   c. The poor man.

SECOND LISTENING: FACTS AND DETAILS

Listen to each part of the lecture again. This time listen to learn more facts and details. Answer the questions below. Write T (true) or F (false) in front of each sentence.

PART 1

1. _____ The poor man was afraid of the Effendi.

2. _____ The poor man stayed outside the restaurant.

3. _____ The poor man paid for the food he ate.

4. _____ The poor man didn't want to go to court alone.

PART 2

1. _____ The judge decided it was reasonable for the rich man to be paid.

2. _____ The Effendi said the poor man was his younger brother.

3. _____ The Effendi gave the rich man a bag of coins.

4. _____ The Effendi solved the poor man's problem.

4 TAKING NOTES

INDICATING CHRONOLOGICAL ORDER

When something is presented in chronological (time) order, the information is organized in the order that events happen. It is organized by time. For example:

Once a poor man visited Nasreddin. Then they talked. Afterwards they left for the court.

The words below are some of the words used to signal chronological order:

once, during, in, on, yesterday, today, later, when, then, next, after, before, afterwards

You can take notes by focusing on these signal words and writing down what happens next.

LISTEN AGAIN

Listen to the lecture again. Write down what happens. Use the phrases below to help you follow the order. When you are finished, read over your notes and underline the signal words. Compare your notes with a classmate's.

One day . . . visited . . .
Yesterday I stopped . . .
I must go . . . today

When the Effendi and the poor man . . .
Then the judge started talking.
After the Effendi heard what the judge said, he . . .
Then the Effendi . . .
Afterwards, the Effendi and the poor man . . .

One day a poor man visited the Effendi.
Yesterday he stopped in front of a restaurant.

REVIEWING THE CONTENT

RETELLING THE STORY

Part of being a good listener is listening in order to recall what you have heard. In this story, you need to have a general understanding of what happened so that you can simply retell the story. Specific details are not really important. You need to focus on how events are organized.

USING YOUR NOTES

Review the notes you have just written. Then read the sentences below. Number them in the correct order. Compare your order with a classmate's. Read the sentences aloud, adding the signal words.

1. The Effendi and the man went to the court. _____

2. The restaurant owner called the judge. _____

3. The Effendi shook a bag of coins. _____

4. The man stopped outside a restaurant. ___1___

5. The judge told the man to pay. _____

6. The restaurant owner said he ate the smell. _____

7. The Effendi said the debt was paid. _____

PREPARING FOR THE TEST

In your next class, you will take a short test on the lecture. Before the test, be sure to review the following questions. Use your notes as you review.

1. Do you know the meaning of the following words?
   a. jingle   **c.** coins   **e.** punished   **g.** upset   **i.** solve
   b. debts   **d.** judge   **f.** elder   **h.** foolish   **j.** court
2. What did the poor man do yesterday?
3. What did the rich man want him to do?
4. How did the Effendi pay the rich man? Was it fair?
5. What does the Effendi teach us in this story?

REVIEW: FINAL LISTENING

Now listen one last time to the lecture. Follow your notes as you listen. If you still have any questions about the lecture, ask your teacher.

TAKING THE TEST

If you have reviewed the material, you should be ready to take the Review Test. Turn to page 103 and answer the questions.

EXPANSION

Look at the picture below. It shows one scene from another Effendi story about food. With a partner, describe what is happening in the picture. What do you think happened before this scene? What will happen next?

THE THIRSTY POCKETS

Now read the story.

One day, the Effendi was invited to a dinner party at his friend's house. His friend had prepared many delicious things to eat. There was soup, rice, meats, and many kinds of fruit. When it was time to eat, the friend told his guests to enjoy themselves and eat freely. They sat down and began to eat. Next to the Effendi was a man who was eating very fast. He was stuffing his mouth and he was stuffing his pockets. He filled his pockets with everything he could reach. The Effendi quietly picked up a teapot and began pouring tea into the man's pocket. The man became very angry. He started shouting at the Effendi. "What are you doing? Are you crazy?" he shouted. "This isn't a funny joke. We are guests in someone else's house!"

"Excuse me," answered the Effendi. "I have done nothing wrong. I saw that your pockets were hungry. I thought they might be thirsty, too."

Answer the following questions, then compare your answers with a classmate's.

1. Where did the Effendi go? What did the friend tell his guests to do?
2. What was the man next to the Effendi doing? What did the Effendi do?
3. Why did the Effendi pour the tea? What lesson did he want to teach the man?
4. Was what the Effendi did fair? Why or why not?

LEARNING DIFFICULTIES: DYSLEXIA

tiem	for	*time*	*chidl*	for	*child*
b	for	*d*	*p*	for	*q*
p	for	*b*	*n*	for	*u*

Some common mistakes of people with dyslexia

1 TOPIC PREVIEW

Have you known any students like this? Anna tries to answer a question, but the wrong words come out. Thomas studies hard for a spelling test and can tell his mother how each word is spelled, but spells every word wrong on the test. Kurt tries to listen in class, but all he can hear is the wind and the birds outside. Marie forgets her lunch, her homework, and her books even though she tries hard to remember them. Now, how are these kids like Albert Einstein, Leonardo da Vinci, and Cher, the movie star? They all share something. They are smart, but they have trouble learning certain skills. They all have dyslexia.

WARM-UP DISCUSSION

In pairs or small groups, discuss these topics with your classmates.

1. Do you know anyone who has difficulty reading or doing mathematics?
2. Do you know any children who can't sit still or pay attention?
3. Have you heard the term *dyslexia* before? What does it mean to you?
4. In your country are there separate classes for children who have difficulty learning? How are the children grouped?

VOCABULARY PREVIEW

Read the following sentences and try to guess the meaning of the words in *italics*.

1. I don't know how to ***deal with*** the problem. I have no idea what to do.
2. On the test, the lowest grade was a 20 and the highest was a 90. That's a ***range*** of 70 points!
3. I can't ***concentrate*** on my homework if the TV is on. I think about the TV shows instead of my homework.
4. She ***inherited*** her blue eyes from her father and her blond hair from her mother. Her father has big blue eyes and her mother has nice blond hair.
5. Just ***estimate*** how many people are here. You don't need to count them.
6. My baby can't talk yet, and sometimes we can't understand what she wants. She gets so ***frustrated.*** She cries and cries.
7. On the test, three children got 75, two got 92, and one got 68. That's an ***average*** score of 79.
8. Dizzy Gillespie is ***considered*** to have been one of the greatest jazz musicians. Many people think he was the best trumpet player in the world.
9. Please ***tune in*** the TV. The picture is terrible! It is very unclear.
10. I tried to tune in my favorite radio station, but the signal kept ***drifting.*** I could hear the station for a few seconds, but then it would disappear.

Now fill in the blanks in the sentences below. Use the correct form of the words from above.

1. There was a 52-point _____range_____ in the test scores. The highest score was a 92 and the lowest was only a 40!

2. The boy tried and tried to ride his new bicycle, but he kept falling off. He became so _____!

3. I _____ that there are about fifty books here, but I'll count them to be sure.

4. The test was very difficult. The _____ score was only 73.

5. Some people _____ Tokyo to be the most expensive city in the world.

6. The little boy kept getting in trouble. No one knew how _____ him.

7. We need a new TV set. We can't _____ in any channels clearly.

8. I'm reading. Please turn down the radio. I can't _____ with that loud music on!

9. If a radio signal _____, it's hard to keep a station tuned in.

10. That girl is a wonderful singer! She must have _____ her skill from her parents. They are both great singers.

WORD NETWORKS

These are some other words and phrases you will hear in the lecture. Read the list. Ask about and discuss any words or phrases you do not know.

Actions
tell the difference between
pay attention
give up
blame (oneself)

People and things
difficulty
standardized intelligence tests
scores
director
computer chips
channels
ability
chalk
researchers
attitudes

Other
basic (mathematics)
smart
dyslexic
mixed up (confused)
hopeless

3 LISTENING TO THE LECTURE

BEFORE YOU LISTEN

You are going to hear a lecture about dyslexia. List three reasons why school might be difficult for a child with dyslexia.

1. _____

2. _____

3. _____

FIRST LISTENING: MAIN IDEAS

Listen to each part of the lecture to find out the main ideas. Circle a, b, or c.

PART 1

1. The main point the speaker makes is that
   a. most boys are considered to have dyslexia.
   b. dyslexic children have a range of problems.
   c. dyslexic children may be unable to concentrate.

2. According to the speaker, dyslexic children often
   a. are considered not as smart as other children.
   b. are not as smart as other children.
   c. score lower on standardized intelligence tests.

PART 2

1. Dr. Levinson calls kids "upside-down" because
   a. they have a wide range of symptoms.
   b. their brains work differently.
   c. they are often misunderstood.

2. Which of the following best describes how Dr. Levinson compares the brain to a TV set?
   a. It has millions of channels to choose from.
   b. You need to change the channels to tune them in.
   c. The channels must be tuned in correctly to work right.

SECOND LISTENING: FACTS AND DETAILS

Listen to each part of the lecture again. This time listen to learn more facts and details. Answer the questions below. Write T (true) or F (false) in front of each sentence.

PART 1

1. _____ About 60 percent of dyslexics have trouble with mathematics.

2. _____ One out of ten boys is dyslexic.

3. _____ Some 85 percent of dyslexic children have a parent with dyslexia.

4. _____ It has been found that dyslexic children have some slight brain damage.

PART 2

1. _____ According to Dr. Levinson, "computer chips" in the brain receive information about what we see and touch.

2. _____ Children with dyslexia have difficulty because the "computer chips" in their brains don't receive signals correctly.

3. _____ Dr. Levinson believes these "computer chips" only control our ability to write, walk, read, and speak.

4. _____ Dr. Levinson believes it is possible for the brain to fix itself.

4 TAKING NOTES

CONNECTING SUPPORTING FACTS TO MAIN IDEAS

Knowing general ideas is not always enough. You know that the general idea from Part 1 is that children with dyslexia have learning difficulties. The general idea from Part 2 is that Dr. Levinson believes dyslexia is caused by the "computer chips" in the brain not working correctly. As you take notes, you need to write down information to support these general ideas. You need to be able to connect supporting details and examples to the main ideas.

LISTEN AGAIN

Listen to the lecture again. This time pay attention to specific examples and facts given. Use the words and phrases below to help you connect the main ideas and the supporting details. Compare your notes with a classmate's.

Part 1
Definition   there are a variety of learning difficulties
Symptoms   problems concentrating; difficulty reading
                         and writing; telling time

Other
background   inherited; more boys have; more boys
                        than girls tested, though

Part 2: Dr. Harold N. Levinson
Theory of cause   computer chips don't tune in signal
                       correctly; it drifts

Attitude
toward education   children with dyslexia are smart; learn
                      differently

REVIEWING THE CONTENT

MAKING INFERENCES

Certain ideas can be concluded or figured out from a lecture. The speaker may not state the idea directly, but you can figure it out from what is said. When you figure out something without full information, this is called *making an inference*. When you make an inference, it is important to be able to identify the specific information the speaker gave and what ideas you have inferred (figured out).

USING YOUR NOTES

Look at the statements below. Which of the statements can we infer from the lecture? Support your answers with information from your notes. Compare your answers with a classmate's. Continue reviewing your notes, making inferences about what you've heard.

1. Dyslexic children generally have a difficult time in school.
2. Dyslexic children are sometimes considered to be less intelligent.
3. School systems often don't know how to teach dyslexics.
4. Dyslexic children don't like school as much as other children.
5. Dyslexic boys have a harder time in school than dyslexic girls.

PREPARING FOR THE TEST

In your next class, you will take a short test on the lecture. Before the test, be sure to review the following questions. Use your notes as you review.

1. Do you know the meaning of the following words?
   a. range   **c.** estimate   **e.** frustrated   **g.** concentrate   **i.** deal with
   b. tune in   **d.** considered   **f.** inherited   **h.** drifting   **j.** average
2. What does it mean to be dyslexic?
3. Why do dyslexic children often have difficulty in school?
4. Who is Dr. Levinson?
5. What is his theory about what causes dyslexia?

REVIEW: FINAL LISTENING

Now listen one last time to the lecture. Follow your notes as you listen. If you still have any questions about the lecture, ask your teacher.

TAKING THE TEST

If you have reviewed the material, you should be ready to take the Review Test. Turn to page 105 and answer the questions.

EXPANSION

It is difficult to understand what it is really like to be dyslexic. One problem some dyslexics have is following the order of letters in a word. They may see *top* as *pot* and *pig* as *gip*. Look at the words below. With a partner, take turns reading them backwards.

LIP　　ABOUT　　SAIL　　WINDOW　　TALL

Now think of five more words. On a separate piece of paper, write the words backwards as shown below. With a partner, exchange papers. Take turns reading each other's words. Talk about how you felt as you tried to read them.

Think of: YELLOW　　　Write: WOLLEY

Read the following news clips. Discuss them with a partner.

NEWS CLIPS

At Harvard University School of Medicine in Boston, Massachusetts, doctors have studied the brains of people with dyslexia. Dr. Albert Galaburda, a professor there, has done research on the way the brain cells are organized. He has learned recently that the cells in the brains of people with dyslexia are organized differently.

If your mother or father has dyslexia, it is much more likely that you also will have it. It's not always easy to know if they have it, though. As people get older, they often learn how to cover up their problems. Sometimes, parents only realize they have it when their children are tested in school. One father said he was always a poor writer. He couldn't spell. After his daughter was tested for dyslexia, he realized he had it, too.

SOURCE: Adapted from Jones, Rhoda Dankin, "Word Muddles, New Theories about Dyslexia." *American Health,* Sept. 1992, 65–69.

SAND PAINTING

 # TOPIC PREVIEW

Native Americans throughout the United States still practice traditional medicine. Sand painting is a very old art done by the Navajo people in the southwestern part of the United States. It is done by a medicine man to help those who are sick. The Navajos believe the world has a certain balance. Everything has its own place. People get sick because they upset the balance of the world. In order for a person to become healthy again, the balance of the world must be restored. The sand-painting ceremony is one way to do this.

WARM-UP DISCUSSION

In pairs or small groups, discuss these topics with your classmates.

1. How do you think a sand painting can make someone healthy?
2. Navajos believe a person is healthy if mind, body, and spirit are in balance. What do you think it means to be healthy?
3. Using a sand painting to heal someone is an example of traditional medicine. In your own culture, what types of traditional medicine are used?

VOCABULARY PREVIEW

Read the following sentences and try to guess the meaning of the words in *italics*.

1. When the doctor got to the office, there were five ***patients*** waiting. They all looked very sick.
2. The priest sang a ***chant*** at the end of the wedding. He sang it over and over to bring good luck to the bride and groom.
3. If you cut your finger badly, it usually takes a long time to ***heal.***
4. Red ***represents*** happiness in some cultures, but it means danger in other cultures.
5. There are many Native American ***tribes*** in North America. Each group has its own way of doing things.
6. The ***symbol*** for No Smoking is a circle around a cigarette with a line through it.
7. The storm ***destroyed*** the house. There was nothing left.
8. I need a ***balance*** of work and play. After work, I do something fun like go to a movie or play tennis.
9. The box of books was too heavy, so I ***transferred*** some books to another box.
10. Our team had five boys and five girls, but the balance has been ***upset.*** Another girl just joined the team.

Now match each word with its correct definition.

1. ___j___ tribes
2. _____ balance
3. _____ symbol
4. _____ represents
5. _____ destroyed
6. _____ upset
7. _____ chant
8. _____ heal
9. _____ patients
10. _____ transferred

a. moved from one place to another
b. make healthy
c. a simple song sung over and over, usually in a religious situation
d. people who are sick
e. stands for; means
f. evenness; equality
g. disturb or change from normal
h. damaged completely
i. something that represents something else
j. groups of people, each with a common name, language, and culture

WORD NETWORKS

These are some other words you will hear in the lecture. Read the list. Ask about and discuss any words you do not know.

Actions
trust
slide
facing (east)
touches
disturb

People and things
ceremony
illnesses
heroes
adventures
gods
cures
bed (of sand)
details
sunset
sunrise
season
dawn
middle age
power

Other
related
holy
powerful
delicate

3 LISTENING TO THE LECTURE

BEFORE YOU LISTEN

You are going to hear a lecture about sand paintings. You will learn about how they are made. Can you guess what the first step is?

FIRST LISTENING: MAIN IDEAS

Listen to each part of the lecture to find out the main ideas. Circle a, b, or c.

PART 1

1. What is the main reason sand paintings are done?
   a. To heal someone.
   b. To find out if someone is sick.
   c. To tell stories about Navajo heroes.

2. First the medicine man decides
   a. what to make a picture of.
   b. what chant to sing.
   c. what the problem is.

PART 2

1. To be sung over means
   a. sand is thrown onto a person.
   b. medicine is thrown over a person.
   c. healing energy is carried to a person.

2. The Navajos believe people become sick because
   a. they upset the world balance.
   b. their diets were not in balance.
   c. they didn't balance work and play.

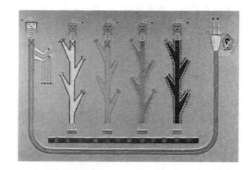

This sand painting uses the five main colors. The cacti, from left to right, are white, yellow, blue, and black. The blossoms on each cactus are red.

SECOND LISTENING: FACTS AND DETAILS

Listen to each part of the lecture again. This time listen to learn more facts and details. Answer the questions below. Write T (true) or F (false) in front of each sentence.

PART 1

1. _____ Anyone can make a sand painting.

2. _____ The medicine man chooses different chants for different illnesses.

3. _____ The sand painting and chant used are about the same story.

4. _____ The medicine man uses a small, wide brush to make the sand painting.

PART 2

1. _____ The patient wears special clothes for the sand-painting ceremony.

2. _____ A sand painting must be made and destroyed within twelve hours.

3. _____ White stands for death.

4. _____ Red means power.

4 TAKING NOTES

LISTING THE STEPS IN A PROCESS

A *process* is how something is done, for example, how to put film in a camera. When someone explains a process, certain words are used to signal the steps to take.

Some of these words are: *first, second, third, after that, afterwards, later, next, then, finally, last, in conclusion.*

In the lecture, the speaker first explains who the medicine man is and what a sand painting is. Then the speaker says: *"It is made as part of a healing ceremony. OK, now here's how it's done."*

This statement, *"here's how it's done,"* is a very important signal for you. It tells you that the speaker is going to describe the steps in making a sand painting. Paying attention to the signal words will make it easier for you to follow the steps.

LISTEN AGAIN

Listen to the lecture again. This time take notes on the steps in making a sand painting. Pay attention to the words the speaker uses to signal the steps. Take notes by dividing a piece of paper into two columns. Make your notes in the right column. Write the signal words in the left column. When you are finished, compare your notes with a classmate's.

| When | When someone becomes sick, the medicine man is called. |
| First | First, the medicine man decides what the problem is. |

5 REVIEWING THE CONTENT

TELLING THE STEPS OF A PROCESS

This lecture tells you the process of making a sand painting. The speaker uses signal words to give the steps. Reviewing the signal words can help you to remember the steps.

USING YOUR NOTES

Look at the lecture notes you have just written. Review the information by covering up the right column. Look at the signal words only. Try to recall each step. Use the phrases below if you need to. Compare your information with a classmate's.

When someone becomes sick, . . .
First, the medicine man must decide . . .
Then, he chooses . . .
After that, he begins to make . . .
When the sand painting is finished, . . .
Next the patient . . .
After the ceremony, . . .

PREPARING FOR THE TEST

In your next class, you will take a short test on the lecture. Before the test, be sure to review the following questions. Use your notes as you review.

1. Do you know the meaning of the following words?
   a. patients **c.** chant **e.** balance **g.** upset **i.** tribes
   b. heal **d.** transferred **f.** represents **h.** symbol **j.** destroyed
2. Who makes a sand painting?
3. Why is it done?
4. How long does it take?
5. What colors are used? What does each represent?

REVIEW: FINAL LISTENING

Now listen one last time to the lecture. Follow your notes as you listen. If you still have any questions about the lecture, ask your teacher.

TAKING THE TEST

If you have reviewed the material, you should be ready to take the Review Test. Turn to page 107 and answer the questions.

EXPANSION

Read the paragraph below. Then answer the questions. Compare your answers with a classmate's.

A sand painting reflects the Navajo's belief in the Great Spirit. They believe the Great Spirit created everything on earth. Every line, every object in a sand painting is a symbol. It represents part of their belief system. For example, look at the figure below. This sand painting represents what the Navajos believe to be the first creation of the Great Spirit: Father Sky and Mother Earth. All life comes from them. In the figure, you see Father Sky on the left, Mother Earth on the right. Notice the letters on the picture. Find A and B. A and B show the places where the hands and feet cross. This represents that heaven and earth—that is, the mind and the body—are one. They work together. Find C on Father Sky. This marks the symbols for the stars and the moon. Locate D on Mother Earth. It marks the sun, which makes all living things grow. The four circles at the top represent the four seasons: summer, fall, winter, and spring.

1. Who are Father Sky and Mother Earth?
2. What do A and B mark?
3. What does C mark? D?
4. What do the four circles at the top represent?
5. In your own culture or religion, is there anyone like Father Sky and Mother Earth?

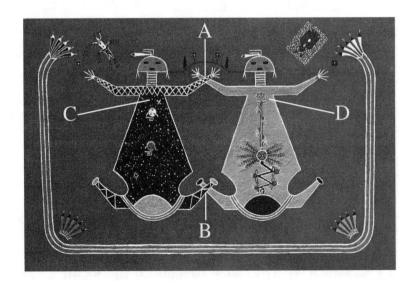

UNIT 7
Physics

SOUND

1 TOPIC PREVIEW

Sounds are all around us. Every day we hear hundreds of sounds at home, in restaurants, in stores, as we walk along the street. What is sound? If we could see a sound wave, what would it look like? Think of throwing a rock into some water. What happens to the water? What does it look like? If we could see a sound wave, it would look like a water wave. What happens to the air in a sound wave?

WARM-UP DISCUSSION

In pairs or small groups, discuss these topics with your classmates.

1. Make a list of ten sounds in a city.
2. Draw a picture of a rock hitting the surface of some water. Show it to a classmate. Talk about what happens to the water and why.
3. Do you know what happens to the air when a sound is made?

VOCABULARY PREVIEW

Read the following sentences and try to guess the meaning of the words in *italics*.

1. The man had a ***series*** of problems. As soon as one problem was gone, he got a new problem.
2. During the earthquake, I could feel the building ***vibrate.*** I could even see it move back and forth.
3. The child ***created*** a beautiful picture. She made it out of colored paper, glue, and string.
4. The wind made a ***pattern*** in the sand. The ***pattern*** looked like ocean waves.
5. I ***store*** my blankets in a box. I keep them there all summer.
6. Our ***original*** plan was to go to a movie, but we changed the plan. We went to dinner instead.
7. The children made ***continuous*** noise. They never stopped all day.
8. The teacher told the students to ***spread out*** in the room. The students moved away from each other.
9. Please don't ***strike*** the bell again. When you hit it before, you woke up the baby.
10. I like the ***area*** of the beach between First and Second Avenue. It's the nicest part.

Now fill in the blanks in the sentences below. Use the correct form of the words from above.

1. The music from my neighbor's apartment was ___continuous___. It never stopped.

2. Don't _____ the dog because she ate your shoe. Hitting her won't fix it.

3. My favorite _____ of this park is near the lake.

4. I liked the _____ *Batman* show better than the new *Batman* show.

5. We had a _____ of thunderstorms last week. There was one storm a day for almost the whole week.

6. Please _____. It's too hot to stand so close together.

7. I _____ my computer files on $3\frac{1}{2}$" disks.

8. We used candles and flowers to _____ a nice feeling at the dinner party.

9. When I use my washing machine, it _____ so hard that it hits the wall.

10. The ice made beautiful _____ on the living room windows.

WORD NETWORKS

These are some other words and phrases you will hear in the lecture. Read the list. Ask about and discuss any words or phrases you do not know.

Actions
thinning out
recording
copied
played back

People and things
air pressure
tuning fork
prongs
molecules
rate
representation
magnetic tape
bits of information
binary codes
melody

Other
neutral
per second
analog
digital
popular

3 LISTENING TO THE LECTURE

BEFORE YOU LISTEN

You are going to hear a lecture about what a sound wave is. How is a sound wave like a water wave?

_____

FIRST LISTENING: MAIN IDEAS

Listen to each part of the lecture to find out the main ideas. Circle a, b, or c.

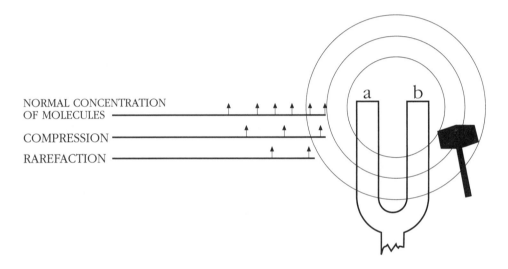

NORMAL CONCENTRATION OF MOLECULES

COMPRESSION

RAREFACTION

PART 1

1. A sound is created by
   a. molecules of air both pushing together and thinning out.
   b. an increased amount of neutral air pressure.
   c. vibrating areas of high air pressure.

2. Another way to say sound wave is
   a. a noise loud enough for us to hear.
   b. molecules of air spreading apart.
   c. a series of air pressure changes.

PART 2

1. The main difference between analog and digital recording is how
   a. the signal affects the microphone.
   b. the microphone is used.
   c. the sound is stored.

2. One way analog and digital recordings are the same is that they
   a. have small bits of information.
   b. are played back as continuous sound.
   c. record the shape of the sound.

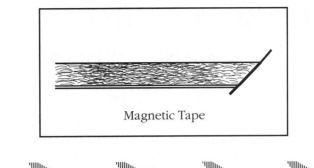

Magnetic Tape

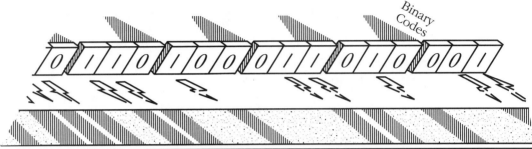

Binary Codes

SECOND LISTENING: FACTS AND DETAILS

Listen to each part of the lecture again. This time listen to learn more facts and details. Answer the questions below. Write T (true) or F (false) in front of each sentence.

PART 1

1. _____ An area of low pressure is a compression.

2. _____ As molecules are compressed, they push together.

3. _____ In a rarefaction there are fewer molecules than before the sound was made.

4. _____ For a sound to be heard, it must have 20 compressions and 20 rarefactions per minute.

PART 2

1. _____ In an analog recording, the sound is copied as a picture.

2. _____ The shape of the magnetism on the tape represents the sound recorded.

3. _____ In digital recording, small pictures of the information are stored.

4. _____ When a digital recording is played, the information is put back together as a continuous sound.

4 TAKING NOTES

MAKING DRAWINGS IN YOUR NOTES

During a lecture, a speaker sometimes asks you to look at a chart, a picture, or a diagram to help you understand the lecture. Some of the signal words and expressions a speaker might use are

look at   find   locate   notice

In this lecture, the speaker says, "Look at the figure on page . . ." This is a signal. You need to look at the figure in order to be able to follow what the speaker will tell you next.

In your notes, it is a good idea to make your own drawing of the figure the speaker refers to. This will help you follow and remember what the speaker says.

LISTEN AGAIN

Listen to the lecture again. Make a drawing to show the parts of a sound wave. When you are finished, compare your drawing with a classmate's. Be sure to include and label:

compression   rarefaction   tuning fork   prongs

REVIEWING THE CONTENT

MAKING COMPARISONS

In the second part of the lecture, the speaker discusses the two main ways of recording sound. It is important to be able to compare these two ways of recording. Some of the expressions we can use to make comparisons are:

but   *however*   *in contrast*   *whereas*

For example:
Analog recording is a picture of the sound, *but* digital recording isn't.

USING YOUR NOTES

Look at the statements below. For each decide if it describes analog (A) or digital (D) recording. On a separate piece of paper, write five comparison sentences.

1. The recording is a picture of the sound.   _____A_____

2. The recording has bits of information.   _____

3. The sound is stored electronically.   _____

4. The sound is stored in a magnetic pattern.   _____

5. The recording has continuous information.   _____

PREPARING FOR THE TEST

In your next class, you will take a short test on the lecture. Before the test, be sure to review the following questions. Use your notes as you review.

1. Do you know the meaning of the following words?
   - **a.** series
   - **b.** store
   - **c.** vibrate
   - **d.** original
   - **e.** created
   - **f.** pattern
   - **g.** strike
   - **h.** continuous
   - **i.** area
   - **j.** spread out
2. What are the three areas of air pressure in a sound wave?
3. What are the two main ways sound is recorded?

REVIEW: FINAL LISTENING

Now listen one last time to the material. Follow your notes as you listen. If you still have any questions about the lecture, ask your teacher.

TAKING THE TEST

Now take the Review Test. Turn to page 109 and answer the questions.

EXPANSION

Read the description of amplitude below. With a partner, take turns explaining what it is. As you listen to your partner, make a drawing to help you understand the information.

AMPLITUDE

The loudness of a sound is called the amplitude. Look at the figure below. The straight line, marked *a*, is the normal air pressure. The curved line, marked *b*, is the pressure above and below normal air pressure that is caused by the sound wave. Find *c* in the figure. *C* marks the crest of the wave. The crest, as you can see, is the highest point of the wave. Now find *d*. *D* marks the trough. The trough is the lowest point of the wave. The amplitude is the difference between compression and the normal air pressure, or between rarefaction and the normal air pressure. We can measure it from the crest of the wave (*c*) to the straight line (*a*), or from the trough of the wave (*d*), to the straight line (*a*).

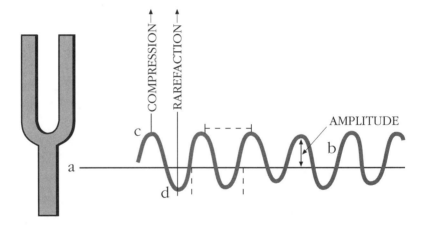

With a partner, discuss the answers to these questions.

1. What makes one sound louder than another sound? Check the answer below.
2. How do you think a sound wave of a loud drum and a sound wave of a whisper compare? Draw what you think the sound waves of each might look like. Compare your drawings with your partner's. If possible, go to a library and check your answers.

DESERTS: THEY KEEP EXPANDING

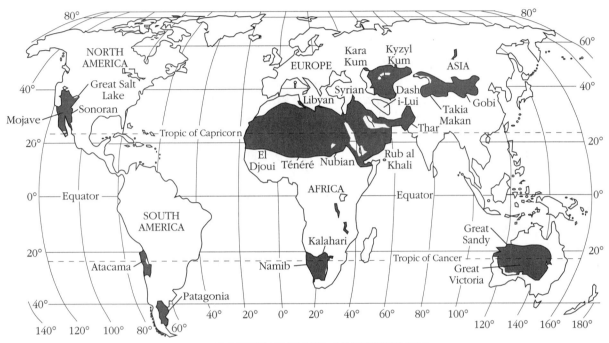

DESERT REGIONS OF THE WORLD

1 TOPIC PREVIEW

There are deserts in many places in the world. As you can see above, most of the large desert areas are near the equator. Deserts are very dry areas with high daytime temperatures and cool nights. There is little rainfall, and few plants or animals can live there. Scientists have found that the world's deserts are spreading and new deserts are appearing. The question is why? Why is the land that is good for raising food and animals being destroyed and disappearing? What can we do to keep this from happening?

WARM-UP DISCUSSION

In pairs or small groups, discuss these topics with your classmates.

1. The Sahara Desert is the largest desert in the world. What do you know about it? What other deserts do you know about?
2. Why do you think the world's deserts are spreading?
3. Why do you think there are new deserts?

VOCABULARY PREVIEW

Read the following sentences and try to guess the meaning of the words in *italics*.

1. Wind and rain badly ***eroded*** the beach. There was hardly any beach left.
2. The land was ***fertile;*** the farmers could grow food easily.
3. The ***soil*** was good for growing melons. It was dry and sandy.
4. ***Topsoil*** is the good, fertile soil at the top of the ground.
5. The sun ***evaporated*** all of the water in the bucket. There was none left.
6. The ground needed more ***moisture.*** It was too dry.
7. The farm was ***productive.*** Many kinds of fruits and vegetables grew there.
8. The cows ***grazed*** all day outside in the fields, then ate more in the barn at night.
9. The farmer used too much ***fertilizer.*** He wanted big plants, but he hurt the soil.
10. The desert has ***spread;*** it's larger this year than last year.

Now match each word with its correct definition.

1. ___*e*___ eroded
2. _____ fertile
3. _____ soil
4. _____ topsoil
5. _____ evaporated
6. _____ moisture
7. _____ productive
8. _____ grazed
9. _____ fertilizer
10. _____ spread

a. get bigger and wider
b. land; ground
c. walked around and ate
d. rich; able to grow a lot of plants
e. washed away
f. went into the air as vapor
g. chemicals used to help plants grow
h. good, rich soil
i. water or liquid in something
j. producing well

WORD NETWORKS

These are some other words you will hear in the lecture. Read the list. Ask about and discuss any words you do not know.

Actions
increasing
decreasing
appearing
manage
take care of
destroyed
mismanaging
pack down

People and things
regions
equator
ground
irrigation
crops

Other
worldwide
agricultural
available

3 LISTENING TO THE LECTURE

BEFORE YOU LISTEN

You are going to hear a lecture about why productive land is disappearing. What do you think the main cause is?

_____

FIRST LISTENING: MAIN IDEAS

Listen to each part of the lecture to find out the main ideas. Circle a, b, or c.

PART 1

1. Large areas of the world now have
   a. more rain and fewer plants.
   b. more moisture.
   c. less rain and fewer plants.

2. According to scientists, the main reason deserts are spreading is
   a. nature.
   b. people.
   c. plants and animals.

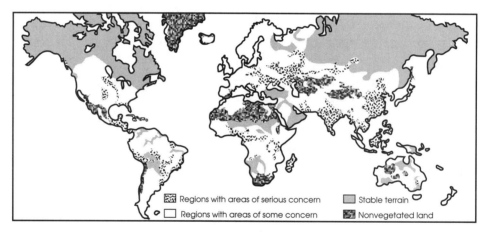

Regions with areas of serious concern   Stable terrain

Regions with areas of some concern   Nonvegetated land

SOURCE: Stroh, M., and J. Raloff. "New UN Soil Survey: The Dirt on Erosion." *Science News,* April 4, 1992, 215.

PART 2

1. Thirty-five percent of topsoil erosion is caused by
   a. overcutting of trees.
   b. overgrazing.
   c. poor farming methods.

2. Losing topsoil is a problem
   a. only in Africa and Asia.
   b. only in the United States.
   c. all over the world.

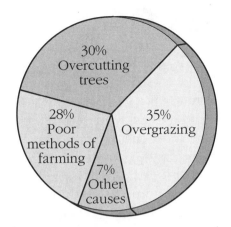

SECOND LISTENING: FACTS AND DETAILS

Listen to each part of the lecture again. This time listen to learn more facts and details. Answer the questions below. Write T (true) or F (false) in front of each sentence.

PART 1

1. _____ Dry, desertlike areas are appearing in many parts of the world.

2. _____ Deserts cannot hold moisture well.

3. _____ Less rain causes more plants to grow.

4. _____ Topsoil erosion makes land less productive.

PART 2

1. _____ Overgrazing means animals don't eat enough plants.

2. _____ If animals pack down the soil, less moisture evaporates.

3. _____ If trees aren't replanted, erosion increases.

4. _____ Poor irrigation can cause too much salt in the soil.

4 TAKING NOTES

USING SHAPES TO TAKE NOTES

Part of learning to take good notes is learning which technique works best for you. You need to ask yourself: Which technique will help me remember information the most easily? Some people are visually oriented. This means they can remember things better if they make pictures and figures. You can use different shapes: a triangle for a three-part idea, a square for a four-point idea. The most important thing is to write down the information in a way that helps you remember it easily.

In this lecture, the speaker talks about three main reasons topsoil is eroding and deserts are increasing. You can take notes about this in the shape of a triangle.

LISTEN AGAIN

Listen to the lecture again. In Part 2, pay attention to the three main reasons given for topsoil erosion. Take notes in the shape of a triangle as shown below. Compare your notes with a classmate's.

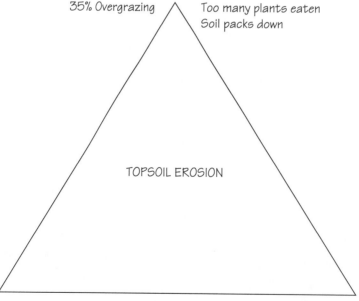

35% Overgrazing   Too many plants eaten
Soil packs down

TOPSOIL EROSION

30% Overcutting of trees   28% Poor methods of farming

REVIEWING THE CONTENT

IDENTIFYING FACTS AND OPINIONS

During a lecture, a speaker usually presents both facts and opinions. It is important to be able to tell the difference. A *fact* is information that is known to be true. People agree it is true. For example, "the Earth is round" is a fact. An *opinion* is an idea. It might be based on observations, but it hasn't been proven.

USING YOUR NOTES

Look at your lecture notes. Review the information. Then look at the sentences below. Decide which are facts (F) and which are opinions (O). Compare your answers with a classmate's.

1. Productive land is decreasing.   _____

2. It's difficult to live in a desert.   _____

3. There is less rain now in some parts of the world.   _____

4. Thirty-five percent of soil erosion is from overgrazing.   _____

5. More people should replant trees to hold the soil.   _____

6. People need to be more careful about cutting down trees.   _____

PREPARING FOR THE TEST

In your next class, you will take a short test on the lecture. Before the test, be sure to review the following questions. Use your notes as you review.

1. Do you know the meaning of the following words?
   a. eroded   **c.** topsoil   **e.** productive   **g.** soil   **i.** evaporated
   b. grazed   **d.** fertile   **f.** moisture   **h.** spread **j.** fertilizer
2. What are the three main reasons for soil erosion?
3. Why is having less productive land a problem?

REVIEW: FINAL LISTENING

Now listen one last time to the lecture. Follow your notes as you listen.

TAKING THE TEST

Now take the Review Test. Turn to page 111 and answer the questions.

EXPANSION

It is not always easy to tell the difference between a fact and an opinion. It is important to pay attention to the information source. Here is an example.

Some people believe that eating meat is very bad for the environment. The National Cattlemen's Association in the United States says that the environmentalists are not telling the truth. They have published a booklet called *Myths and Facts about Beef Production*. They say the environmentalists' ideas are myths, and their own ideas are the facts. Who should we believe?

Below are a few examples from the booklet. Read the information. In pairs or small groups, discuss these questions:

1. Who do you think is right? Why do you think there is such a big difference in what they are saying?
2. What could you do to find out more about this?

FOOD RESOURCES

Myth: By eating less meat, we could use our natural resources better. More land and water and other resources would be available for other food crops rather than meat.

Fact: We use our natural resources best by raising both animals (beef) *and* plant crops. This is because half of the land in the United States is only good for grazing. It isn't good for growing food crops. The land wouldn't be used at all if it were not used for grazing.

TOPSOIL EROSION

Myth: Livestock cause a lot of topsoil erosion. Overgrazing in the western part of the United States is largely responsible for topsoil erosion.

Fact: Cattle are not a major cause of topsoil erosion in the United States. Using grazing animals to produce food conserves, in other words, saves the soil. This is because the animals eat what grows naturally. Farm land is not used to provide them food. Experts agree that the grazing areas of the United States are in better condition now than they were 100 years ago.

TREES

Myth: Beef cattle cause trees to be cut down (deforestation) in the United States and in Central America.

Fact: Beef cattle aren't important in deforestation in the United States or in Central America. Only .4% of the beef eaten in the United States comes from Central America anyway.

SOURCE: Adapted from Glidden, Judith. "Cattlemen's Group: Opponents Skew the Facts." *The Minuteman Chronicle,* November 7, 1992, 1, 8.

PHOTOGRAPHS TODAY: DO THEY TELL THE TRUTH?

How are they different?

1 TOPIC PREVIEW

A newspaper decides to smooth the skin of a woman and make her eyes a little bluer before they print her picture. They decide to take a tree out of a picture of the queen of England because the picture would be better without it. They also decide to remove a can of beer from a famous basketball player's hand because the public doesn't want to see an athlete drinking beer. Is it all right to change photographs to increase newspaper sales? The basic question is: When is it acceptable to change a photograph? When is changing a photograph the same thing as changing the news? What should the rules be?

WARM-UP DISCUSSION

In pairs or small groups, discuss these topics with your classmates.

1. What kinds of changes to photographs do you think are all right?
2. Imagine that the president was sick in the hospital. For what reasons do you think it would be all right to change a photograph taken there?
3. Do you know of any examples of photographs being changed in magazines or newspapers in your own country?

2 VOCABULARY PREVIEW

Read the following sentences and try to guess the meaning of the words in *italics*.

1. This is an ***ethical*** question: Is it okay to take from the rich to help the poor?
2. We had to ***alter*** our vacation plans. We had planned to stay in Hawaii for one week, but we had to change our plans because our son got very sick.
3. The family ***faced*** many problems: Their house burned down, they needed money, and their car wouldn't run.
4. There are many ***events*** planned for the summer festival: a dance, a picnic, a boat race, and a baseball game.
5. Can you ***prove*** that man stole your money? Can you show it's true?
6. This watch is ***worth*** a lot of money. It is made of gold.
7. There are two ***basic*** ways to lose weight: Eat less and exercise more.
8. That movie is ***based on*** a book by Stephen King, but it's really different from the book.
9. If I ***manipulate*** the numbers in my checkbook, it looks like I have more money than I really have.
10. I went to a computer ***training*** class last year. We learned a lot in one week.

Now fill in the blanks in the sentences below. Use the correct form of the words from above.

1. Some people can't ___face___ the fact that if they want to lose weight, they need to eat less.

2. I don't think it is ever _____ to steal something, even if it helps someone else.

3. My favorite _____ in the Olympics is the women's gymnastics.

4. Your new sportscar must be _____ a lot of money! It looks expensive.

5. I am worried that Thomas is so late, _____ the fact that he is always on time.

6. The police needed to _____ the man stole the money from the bank.

7. If you _____ the antenna on your TV, you'll get a better picture.

8. I need to _____ this jacket. The sleeves are too long.

9. Food, clothing, and a place to live are the _____ things we all need.

10. You need a lot of _____ to be a doctor. You have to go to school for many years.

WORD NETWORKS

These are some other words and phrases you will hear in the lecture. Read the list. Ask about and discuss any words or phrases you do not know.

Actions
lie
admit

People and things
technology
parades
prime minister
frowns
truth
proof
media
rules
National Geographic
pyramids
Time magazine
studio
American Embassy
responsibility

Other
available
believable
Egyptian

3 LISTENING TO THE LECTURE

BEFORE YOU LISTEN

You are going to hear a lecture about photojournalism. What is the job of a photojournalist?

FIRST LISTENING: MAIN IDEAS

Listen to each part of the lecture to find out the main ideas. Circle a, b, or c.

PART 1

1. The example of the picture of the president and prime ministers shows us
   a. most photographers try to change their photos.
   b. some of the ways photographs can be changed.
   c. altering photographs isn't new.

2. The main problem with electronic imaging is
   a. it makes changes that are difficult to notice.
   b. computers are difficult to use for changing photographs.
   c. you need special training to change photographs.

PART 2

1. "Photographs don't lie" means
   a. we can tell a photo has been changed.
   b. photographs are changed more nowadays.
   c. photographs tell us what really happened.

2. The reaction to what *National Geographic* did in 1982 shows us
   a. photographs can easily be changed.
   b. people don't like being fooled.
   c. it is possible to move the pyramids.

SECOND LISTENING: FACTS AND DETAILS

Listen to each part of the lecture again. This time listen to learn more facts and details. Answer the questions below. Write T (true) or F (false) in front of each sentence.

PART 1

1. _____ The speaker thinks a photojournalist's job is to give us the real news.

2. _____ Changing photographs has only been done recently.

3. _____ To do electronic imaging requires a lot of special training.

4. _____ Electronic imaging can take someone out of a photograph.

PART 2

1. _____ The speaker feels people want to be able to believe photographs.

2. _____ Newspapers and magazines now follow the same rules.

3. _____ *Time* magazine tried to make it look like their photograph had been taken in Moscow.

4. _____ The speaker believes photojournalists should use electronic imaging to get the effect they want.

4 TAKING NOTES

MAKING A WEB

One interesting way to take notes is to make a web (like a spider's web) to show how the ideas in the lecture are connected.

To do this, you draw a circle. You write the lecture topic in the center of the circle. For this lecture, write "Photojournalism: Using electronic imaging" inside the circle.

Make lines coming out from the circle. On these lines, write the main ideas you hear.

LISTEN AGAIN

Listen to the lecture again. Take notes in a web using the model shown below. Add more lines for other ideas you want to write down. Compare your notes with a classmate's.

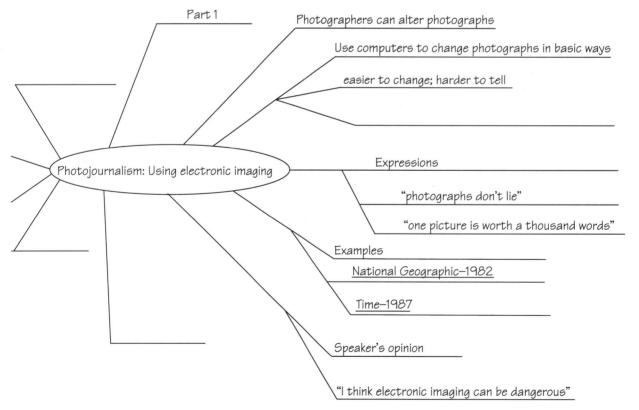

REVIEWING THE CONTENT

REPORTING SOMEONE'S POINT OF VIEW

In this lecture, the speaker expresses a point of view regarding the use of electronic imaging by photojournalists. You can talk about this as a *direct quote*:

The speaker said, *"I personally think that electronic imaging can be dangerous."* or as *reported speech*:

The speaker said that he thought electronic imaging could be dangerous. In presenting someone's point of view, we often use reported speech.

USING YOUR NOTES

Look at the lecture notes you have just written. Find examples of opinions and points of view of the speaker. Present them to a partner, using the phrase *The speaker said that* . . .

PREPARING FOR THE TEST

In your next class, you will take a short test on the lecture. Before the test, be sure to review the following questions. Use your notes as you review.

1. Do you know the meaning of the following words?
   a. faced   **c.** ethical   **e.** events   **g.** worth   **i.** based on
   b. prove   **d.** manipulate   **f.** alter   **h.** basic   **j.** training
2. How can electronic imaging be used to alter photographs?
3. How is electronic imaging different from how photos were changed in the past?
4. What did *National Geographic* do? *Time* magazine?
5. Does the speaker think electronic imaging should be used by photojournalists?

REVIEW: FINAL LISTENING

Now listen one last time to the lecture. Follow your notes as you listen. If you still have any questions about the lecture, ask your teacher.

TAKING THE TEST

If you have reviewed the material, you should be ready to take the Review Test. Turn to page 113 and answer the questions.

EXPANSION

Video cameras have also had an effect on photojournalism. They can bring us the action, the excitement, and the sounds of the event that the photographer wants to share with us. Whether it is of a marketplace, a car show, or a war scene, video cameras can bring us a fuller picture of what goes on than regular still cameras can.

They can also be used to bring us still photographs similar to those taken with a regular still camera. One technique used is known as *frame grabbing.* With frame grabbing, a picture is taken directly off the TV and used in a newspaper or magazine. The photographer uses a video camera to take a picture from the TV instead of going to where the event is actually taking place. It only takes a few minutes to take a picture and put it into a newspaper. This technique makes it easy for a newspaper to cover the news quickly because no film has to be processed. In addition, the photographer does not have to travel anywhere to take the picture.

There are different opinions about using video cameras this way. Some people feel this use of video cameras is good. They say it is a quick, inexpensive, and efficient way of bringing people the news. Other people do not like it. They say it is secondhand news. By this they mean that someone else, in other words, the person who took the photograph for TV, has already decided what is important and what is not important. They say this makes the news that is available to people more limited than in the past.

YOU DECIDE

In small groups, list the advantages and disadvantages of using video cameras in the way described above. Think about what the job of a newspaper is. Use your imagination. When you are finished, compare your ideas with another group's.

Advantages:

Disadvantages:

ALLERGIES

TOPIC PREVIEW

A person with an allergy is very sensitive to something that does not cause problems for most people. Cats, dogs, feathers, plants, pollen, dust, and certain foods such as milk and eggs are common things to be allergic to. People may cough or sneeze or have a runny nose if they come in contact with these things. Some people are also allergic to insect stings, for example, bee stings. A bee sting can be very serious for someone who is allergic to it.

WARM-UP DISCUSSION

In pairs or small groups, discuss these topics with your classmates.

1. Are you allergic to anything?
2. Do you know anyone else who is allergic to something? What happens?
3. What can people do if they are allergic to something?

2 VOCABULARY PREVIEW

Read the following sentences and try to guess the meaning of the words in *italics*.

1. The girl was ***slightly*** taller than her friend; only about $\frac{1}{2}$ inch taller.
2. The nurse used a small needle to ***inject*** medicine into the baby's arm.
3. The snake's ***venom*** is so strong, one drop is enough to kill you.
4. A bee ***sting*** feels like a sharp needle in your skin.
5. Our ***immune system*** protects our body from things that can hurt us.
6. My sister's ***immunity*** to colds is great. She hasn't had a cold in five years!
7. When you get sick, your body makes ***antibodies*** to make you well again.
8. When I broke my arm, the ***swelling*** was terrible! My arm got bigger every second!
9. After the woman hurt her head, she was very ***confused.*** She didn't know where she was or how she got there.
10. The child was ***sensitive*** to sunlight. After only a few minutes outside, she was very red.

Now fill in the blanks in the sentences below. Use the correct form of the words from above.

1. If we didn't have an ___immune system___, we would always get sick.

2. I'm _____ older than my best friend. My birthday is two days before hers.

3. Some snakes have _____, but some snakes aren't poisonous.

4. Sometimes when I wake up in the middle of the night, I'm very

   _____. I don't know where I am.

5. It's a good idea to put ice on a broken bone to keep the _____ down until you get to the hospital.

6. Your body makes _____ to protect you and keep you healthy.

7. By getting shots as babies, children have _____ to many diseases.

8. I am _____ to chocolate. It makes me sneeze.

9. A _____ on the hand can really hurt!

10. Needles are used to _____ medicine.

WORD NETWORKS

These are some other words and phrases you will hear in the lecture. Read the list. Ask about and discuss any words or phrases you do not know.

Actions
sneeze
breathing

People and things
bee
runny nose
pain
blood pressure
poison
bump
childhood diseases
measles

Other
itchy
difficulty

3 LISTENING TO THE LECTURE

BEFORE YOU LISTEN

You are going to hear a lecture about allergies and reactions to bee stings. A bee sting can be very dangerous. Do you know why?

FIRST LISTENING: MAIN IDEAS

Listen to each part of the lecture to find out the main ideas. Circle a, b, or c.

PART 1

1. In an allergic reaction, your antibodies
   a. fight other antibodies in your body.
   b. fight your immune system.
   c. fight something that is not a problem for most people.

2. Which of the following best describes an anaphylactic reaction?
   a. a red spot where the sting occurs
   b. pain and swelling all over the body
   c. sharp pain where the sting occurs

PART 2

1. To do a skin test, a doctor puts bee venom
   a. under the skin.
   b. on the skin.
   c. on several parts of the body.

2. Allergy shots make someone less sensitive by
   a. increasing the shots.
   b. increasing reactions.
   c. increasing immunity.

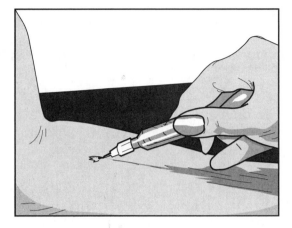

SECOND LISTENING: FACTS AND DETAILS

Listen to each part of the lecture again. This time listen to learn more facts and details. Answer the questions below. Write T (true) or F (false) in front of each sentence.

PART 1

1. _____ In an allergic reaction, the antibodies are confused about what is dangerous.

2. _____ Sneezing and red, itchy eyes are allergic reactions.

3. _____ A normal reaction to a bee sting is pain and difficulty breathing.

4. _____ A general, anaphylactic reaction lasts a short time.

PART 2

1. _____ During an allergy test, the doctor checks the skin color and the size of the bump.

2. _____ A large, red bump usually means someone is slightly allergic.

3. _____ Allergy shots increase an allergic reaction.

4. _____ The doctor decreases the amount of the venom with each shot.

4 TAKING NOTES

USING THE INTRODUCTION TO ORGANIZE YOUR NOTES

A speaker often tells you at the beginning of the lecture how the lecture will be organized. The introduction often gives important help about what to listen for. It can help you concentrate on what the speaker thinks are the main points of the lecture.

Here, the speaker explains you will first hear about allergic reactions, then testing, and finally allergy shots. This gives you a map in your head. You know from the beginning that three key ideas will be covered:

allergic reactions   testing   allergy shots

You can divide your notes into these three sections.

LISTEN AGAIN

Listen to the lecture again. This time pay attention to the three key ideas. Use the three sections below to help you take notes. Compare your notes with a classmate's.

ALLERGIC REACTIONS
—General
—Bee
TESTING
ALLERGY SHOTS
—Why
—How

REVIEWING THE CONTENT

IDENTIFYING MAIN IDEAS

It is necessary to be able to understand the speaker's main purpose or goal. This lecture is divided into three sections.

For each section, ask yourself:

What is the speaker trying to tell me?
What is the purpose of this section?
What would be a good heading for this section?

USING YOUR NOTES

Look at the lecture notes you have just written. For each section, decide what the main ideas are, what the purpose is, and what a good heading would be. Compare your ideas with a classmate's.

PREPARING FOR THE TEST

In your next class, you will take a short test on the lecture. Before the test, be sure to review the following questions. Use your notes as you review.

1. Do you know the meaning of the following words?
   a. immunity   **c.** inject   **e.** immune system   **g.** antibodies   **i.** sensitive
   b. swelling   **d.** sting   **f.** venom   **h.** slightly   **j.** confused
2. What is an allergic reaction?
3. What is a normal reaction to a bee sting?
4. What is an allergic reaction to a bee sting?
5. How does a doctor test for allergies?
6. Why are allergy shots given?

REVIEW: FINAL LISTENING

Now listen one last time to the lecture. Follow your notes as you listen. If you still have any questions about the lecture, ask your teacher.

TAKING THE TEST

If you have reviewed the material, you should be ready to take the Review Test. Turn to page 115 and answer the questions.

EXPANSION

FOOD ALLERGIES

Some people have food allergies. Many of these people are allergic to cow's milk and corn. They should try not to eat them. Milk and corn are actually in many foods sold at the grocery store, however.

Milk
Can be in breads, soups, crackers, meats, hot dogs, desserts, and breakfast cereals. Ingredients on a food label that may mean milk are:

nonfat dried solids	lactose	casein
whey	sodium caseinate	yogurt
curds	lactate	cream

Corn
Can be in chewing gum, margarine, catsup, spaghetti sauce, vitamin pills, toothpaste, aspirin, cough medicine, stamps, and envelopes. Ingredients on a food label that may mean corn are:

corn syrup	cornstarch	sweeteners
corn sweeteners	dextrose	glucose

Look at the following labels. For each, decide with a partner why these foods would not be OK for a person with an allergy to milk or corn.

Crackers
Ingredients: wheat flour, rice flour, vegetable oil, sesame seeds, salt, corn syrup, whey, and leavening

---

Salad dressing
Ingredients: soybean oil, vinegar, water, corn sweeteners, cream, pepper, salt, and flavorings

---

Soup
Ingredients: water, tomatoes, potatoes, carrots, onions, peas, sugar, salt, nonfat solids, spices, and flavorings

---

Check other food labels at home or at a grocery store to see if they would be OK as well.

WORLD MUSIC

1 TOPIC PREVIEW

People sometimes say that the world is getting smaller. By this they mean it feels smaller because we have so much information about what goes on all over the world each day. It is certainly smaller when it comes to music. There is a great variety of music easily available to us each day. At stores and concerts, and on tapes and CDs, we can enjoy music from all over the world. Current technology has made it easy for us to learn about and enjoy new musical styles from parts of the world we have never been to.

WARM-UP DISCUSSION

In pairs or small groups, discuss these topics with your classmates.

1. What type of music do you like?
2. Do you play a musical instrument? If not, did you play when you were younger? Does anyone in your family play a musical instrument?
3. Who is your favorite musician in your country?
4. Who is your favorite musician or musical group from another country?

2 VOCABULARY PREVIEW

Read the following sentences and try to guess the meaning of the words in *italics*.

1. The concert tickets were ***affordable.*** They were so inexpensive that many people could go to the concert.
2. The child was ***passive.*** He just sat there and waited for something to happen.
3. I need ***access*** to the room upstairs that is locked. Can you help me get in?
4. Your idea is ***unique.*** I've never heard one like it before.
5. I ***accelerated*** my exercise schedule so that I would be ready for the ski season. I used to exercise three times a week, but now I do it every day.
6. Going to a concert once a month has ***enriched*** my life; my life is more enjoyable now.
7. The disease was a ***local*** problem. Our town was the only place that had it.
8. I like ***amateur*** sports better than professional sports. Amateur players seem to enjoy the game more than players who get paid.
9. The ***transmission*** of the disease was very fast. On Monday only one child had it, but by Wednesday ten children were sick.
10. You can ***rely on*** me to return your book. I always do what I say.

Now fill in the blanks in the sentences below. Use the correct form of the words from above.

1. Radio and television are good ways to ensure rapid ___transmission___ of news from one part of the world to another part.

2. Can I _____ you to finish this report? I have to have it done.

3. I wouldn't call that restaurant _____. It cost me half of my weekly pay to eat there with a friend.

4. Don't be so _____! If you really want to see the movie, let's go!

5. That is a _____ dress. I've never seen another one like it.

6. She's only an _____ singer, but she sings as well as a professional.

7. To pay off my car faster, I _____ my payments from once to twice a month.

8. I need _____ to a book on Chinese history for my school report. Do you know where I can get one?

9. Having a new theater in town has certainly _____ everyone's life.

10. We have a good _____ hospital. It's just a few minutes from my house.

WORD NETWORKS

These are some other words and phrases you will hear in the lecture. Read the list. Ask about and discuss any words or phrases you do not know.

People and things
memory
village
American bluegrass
Balinese classical
reggae
pop charts

Other
limited
negative (effects)
popular
Arabic
Caribbean
African
traditional

3 LISTENING TO THE LECTURE

BEFORE YOU LISTEN

You are going to hear a lecture about the spread of musical styles around the world. What music from other countries do you listen to?

FIRST LISTENING: MAIN IDEAS

Listen to each part of the lecture to find out the main ideas. Circle a, b, or c.

PART 1

1. According to the speaker, music today is
    a. not as good as it was before recorded music.
    b. not available to most people.
    c. all around us.

2. According to the speaker, the spread of music leads to this negative effect. The speaker means that
    a. we listen to too many kinds of music.
    b. we rely too much on professionals to make music for us.
    c. we spend too much money on music and musical equipment.

PART 2

1. The speaker thinks the accelerated spread of musical styles
    a. will create a new musical richness.
    b. will make music everywhere sound the same.
    c. will weaken the music available to us.

2. World Music is based on
    a. listening to local music.
    b. combining different musical styles.
    c. Paul Simon and Sunny Ade.

SECOND LISTENING: FACTS AND DETAILS

Listen to each part of the lecture again. This time listen to learn more facts and details. Answer the questions below. Write T (true) or F (false) in front of each sentence.

PART 1

1. _____ The speaker says the transmission of music is limited by our memory.

2. _____ One reason music is more available is that sound equipment is too expensive.

3. _____ The speaker feels too many people hear music but don't really listen to it.

4. _____ The speaker believes most people don't play music because they rely on professional musicians instead.

PART 2

1. _____ An Italian music store selling popular Italian music is an example of the spread of musical styles.

2. _____ Paul Simon's use of traditional African sounds on *Graceland* is an example of the spread of musical styles.

3. _____ Sunny Ade and Manu Dibango play local Brazilian music.

4. _____ *A World Out of Time* was recorded in only two weeks.

TAKING NOTES

USING ABBREVIATIONS

Your notes need to be short and clear. One way to do this is to develop a system of abbreviations. You can use the same abbreviations in all of your lecture notes. For example, you can decide to write:

with as *w/* or *between* as *btwn*

You can also create abbreviations for a particular lecture. You can do this for the words that are repeated often. This will save you time and allow you to focus on the important ideas.

For this lecture, the following abbreviations could be used:

rec mu = recorded music   *PS = Paul Simon*

WM = World Music   *loc mu = local music*   *pros = professionals*

LISTEN AGAIN

Listen to the lecture again. Take notes using abbreviations. Before you begin, divide your paper into two columns. Write your notes in the right column as shown below. When you are finished, check your abbreviations. Make sure you know what they mean; otherwise, it will be difficult for you to remember what the lecture was about. Then compare your notes with a classmate's.

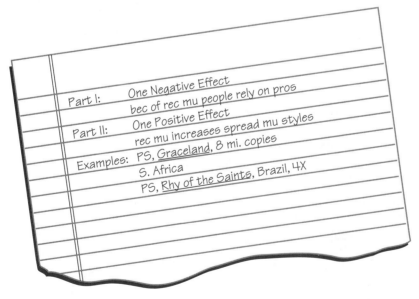

Part I: One Negative Effect
            bec of rec mu people rely on pros

Part II: One Positive Effect
            rec mu increases spread mu styles

Examples: PS, Graceland, 8 mi. copies
           S. Africa
           PS, Rhy of the Saints, Brazil, 4X

REVIEWING THE CONTENT

UNDERSTANDING CAUSE AND EFFECT

When something happens, there is a result. For example, if you wake up late, then you may be late for class. Waking up is the cause. The effect is that you are late. Sometimes, words are used to signal this, for example, *if . . . , then. . . .* Other times, you as a listener have to try to understand the relationship.

This lecture talks about how the ability to record music has had a big impact on the spread of musical styles. The lecture gives you a number of cause and effect relationships that aren't stated directly. For example:

If CD players aren't expensive, *then* more people can buy them.
If stores in Paris sell Caribbean music, *then* French people can become familiar with reggae.

USING YOUR NOTES

Look through the lecture notes you have just written. Then write some sentences showing cause and effect using *if . . . , then. . . .* Compare your sentences with a classmate's.

PREPARING FOR THE TEST

In your next class, you will take a short test on the lecture. Before the test, be sure to review the following questions. Use your notes as you review.

1. Do you know the meaning of the following words?
   - **a.** affordable
   - **b.** enriched
   - **c.** rely on
   - **d.** unique
   - **e.** accelerated
   - **f.** transmission
   - **g.** access
   - **h.** local
   - **i.** passive
   - **j.** amateur
2. What are some of the general effects of recorded music?
3. Why does the speaker think there are fewer amateur musicians?
4. What is World Music? What are two examples of it?
5. What is the speaker's opinion of World Music?

REVIEW: FINAL LISTENING

Now listen one last time to the lecture. Follow your notes as you listen. If you still have any questions about the lecture, ask your teacher.

TAKING THE TEST

If you have reviewed the material, you should be ready to take the Review Test. Turn to page 117 and answer the questions.

EXPANSION

Read the questions below. Interview two students in the class. Write down their answers in the space provided. Then form a small group with other students. Report what you found out.

QUESTIONNAIRE

What kind of music do you like?

Student 1 _____

Student 2 _____

Who is your favorite singer?

Student 1 _____

Student 2 _____

What is your favorite group?

Student 1 _____

Student 2 _____

In your own country, when do you hear live music?

Student 1 _____

Student 2 _____

Did you play a musical instrument when you were young?

Student 1 _____

Student 2 _____

Do you play a musical instrument now?

Student 1 _____

Student 2 _____

Do you own a CD player? A tape recorder?

Student 1 _____

Student 2 _____

What examples of World Music do you know and like?

Student 1 _____

Student 2 _____

PREVENTING DISASTERS

1 TOPIC PREVIEW

Any big storm, or an earthquake, or a volcano erupting can cause a lot of damage and a lot of problems. They are all examples of natural hazards. There are many natural hazards all over the world. As technology improves, scientists can collect more information about natural hazards before they happen. How can governments and scientists work together to use this information? What can they do to help people prepare before a natural hazard so that there is less damage and fewer problems?

WARM-UP DISCUSSION

In pairs or small groups, discuss these topics with your classmates.

1. Can you think of other examples of natural hazards around the world? Make a list.
2. What are three things a city or country can do to prepare for a big storm?
3. Do any natural hazards, such as earthquakes, occur in your country? If the answer is yes, does the government have a plan for dealing with them?

VOCABULARY PREVIEW

Read the following sentences and try to guess the meaning of the words in *italics*.

1. The heavy rains in Bangladesh caused a ***disaster:*** Over 50,000 people died. In addition, homes, animals, and crops were lost.
2. The townspeople ***recovered*** slowly from the storm; day by day their lives returned to normal.
3. The police couldn't ***control*** the angry students. The students kept throwing rocks and shouting no matter what the police did.
4. When Mount Pinatubo ***erupted*** in 1991, it threw a lot of ash into the air.
5. It's a fire ***hazard*** to have curtains near a stove. They can catch fire when you cook.
6. A big fire ***swept*** through the mountains. It moved so quickly that thousands of trees were burned in only a few hours.
7. My friend has a lot of ***property:*** She owns two houses, three cars, and many, many other things.
8. The strong wind broke windows, lifted trees, and hit houses and bridges. The ***destruction*** was terrible.
9. ***Cooperation*** is important. People need to learn how to work together.
10. There are good schools in our ***community.*** The people who live here think education is important.

Now fill in the blanks in the sentences below. Use the correct form of the words from above.

1. Earthquakes are a _____hazard_____ in many parts of Japan.

2. It took a lot of time and money for the town to _____ from the hurricane.

3. Mount Vesuvius _____ in A.D. 79.

4. The fire fighters made a road to _____ the fire, but they couldn't stop it.

5. Spring flooding caused a _____ for the towns near the river. Many houses and businesses were destroyed.

6. Heavy winds from the hurricane _____ through the town breaking many windows.

7. We need the _____ of all students to get the room ready for the party.

8. My brother's car is the only _____ he owns.

9. About 100,000 people live in our _____.

10. The _____ from the earthquake cost the country millions of dollars.

WORD NETWORKS

These are some other words you will hear in the lecture. Read the list. Ask about and discuss any words you do not know.

Actions
damaged
destroyed

People and things
plan
nature
hurricanes
droughts
wildfires
floods
mudflows
phases
maps
routes

Other
complicated
emergency (plan)

3 LISTENING TO THE LECTURE

BEFORE YOU LISTEN

You are going to hear a lecture about planning for natural hazards such as earthquakes. What should a good plan include? List three things.

1. _____ 2. _____ 3. _____

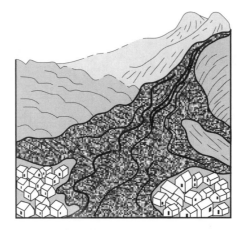

FIRST LISTENING: MAIN IDEAS

Listen to each part of the lecture to find out the main ideas. Circle a, b, or c.

PART 1

1. According to the speaker, we can keep natural hazards from becoming disasters by
   a. controlling them.
   b. moving away from them.
   c. planning for them.

2. The speaker's main point about Nevado del Ruiz is:
   a. Towns were lost and many, many people were killed.
   b. Scientists and governments need to work together.
   c. The scientists marked areas of danger in advance.

PART 2

1. Having a general plan requires first
   a. gathering general scientific information.
   b. deciding where the money will come from.
   c. making a strong emergency plan.

2. A good general plan should include
   a. only detailed emergency routes for the country.
   b. what to do before, during, and after a hazard occurs.
   c. only specific scientific information for that place.

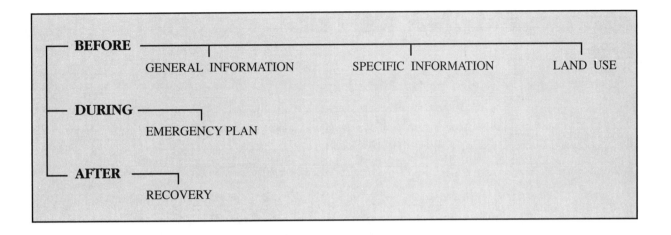

SECOND LISTENING: FACTS AND DETAILS

Listen to each part of the lecture again. This time listen to learn more facts and details. Answer the questions below. Write T (true) or F (false) in front of each sentence.

PART 1

1. _____ Hurricanes, droughts, and flooding are given as examples of natural disasters.

2. _____ According to the speaker, natural disasters can be avoided.

3. _____ Nevado del Ruiz erupted in 1895.

4. _____ Volcanic ice flows caused 25,000 people to die.

PART 2

1. _____ If Colombian scientists study the past, they may be better able to understand what might happen in the future.

2. _____ The main goal of land-use planning discussed here is to have people use as little land as possible for their businesses.

3. _____ The Colombian government didn't know where it was dangerous to live.

4. _____ The speaker says scientists agree that Colombia needed to improve its emergency plan.

4 TAKING NOTES

CLASSIFICATION

A classification divides things into groups. A classification is used to talk about groups of things, people, and places. Some of the signal words a speaker might use are:

categories   *kinds*   *groups*   *types*   *classes*   *areas*

Here the speaker talks about five areas of a general plan. This is a way of classifying and organizing the information. To take notes, you can divide a piece of paper into the number of categories to be presented.

LISTEN AGAIN

Listen to the lecture again. This time pay attention to the five areas of a general plan. Before you listen, divide a piece of paper into five sections using the model below. Compare your notes with a classmate's.

1. General information
   background information from all over the world
2. Specific information
3. Land-use planning
4. Emergency plan
5. Recovery

REVIEWING THE CONTENT

ASKING QUESTIONS

When you read your notes after a lecture, you often have new questions about the topic. You think of things you want to learn more about. One way to review your notes is to read over them and have a conversation with yourself as you go along. Allow yourself to ask questions: *I wonder why. . . ? I'd like to know why. . . . Do/Does . . . ?*

You can find answers to the questions yourself or you can talk to the teacher. It's important to remember that a teacher wants you to ask questions. It's one way the teacher finds out what you have understood and what needs to be explained a little bit more.

USING YOUR NOTES

Look at the lecture notes you have just written. Go through your notes carefully and ask yourself the following questions:

1. What other natural hazards are there in Colombia?
2. Why couldn't the Colombian government use the maps the scientists made?
3. Does Colombia have an emergency plan now?

Talk about your answers with a classmate.

PREPARING FOR THE TEST

In your next class, you will take a short test on the lecture. Before the test, be sure to review the following questions. Use your notes as you review.

1. Do you know the meaning of the following words?
   a. disaster **c.** recovered   **e.** control   **g.** property   **i.** erupted
   b. swept   **d.** cooperation **f.** community   **h.** destruction **j.** hazard
2. What are examples of natural hazards?
3. What lesson was learned at Nevado del Ruiz?
4. What are the five parts of the general plan mentioned in the lecture?
5. What is included in an emergency plan?

REVIEW: FINAL LISTENING

Now listen one last time to the lecture. Follow your notes as you listen. If you still have any questions about the lecture, ask your teacher.

TAKING THE TEST

If you have reviewed the material, you should be ready to take the Review Test. Turn to page 119 and answer the questions.

EXPANSION

THE RING OF FIRE

Volcanoes, on the average, erupt just as often now as they have in the past, but the impact is greater now. More people are killed and more property is lost than in the past. The main reason for this is that the world population has increased. There is not enough safe land for people to live on. It is estimated that about 360 million people live on or near volcanoes.

Look at the map below. It shows the Ring of Fire. The Ring of Fire is a chain of active volcanoes in a belt around the Pacific Ocean. As you can see on the map, it extends from South America up through North America, then down through Japan and the Pacific Ocean to New Zealand.

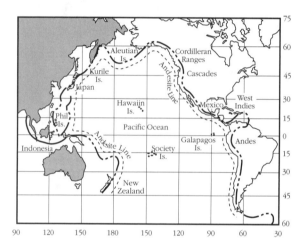

PAIR WORK

Start at one end of the volcano chain. With your finger, follow along the ring. In each continent or country, try to think of the names of cities and large population areas that are on or near the Ring of Fire. Make a list.

GROUP WORK

With another pair, compare lists. Then discuss the following questions.

1. Should governments let people live in areas where there are active volcanoes? List the reasons why they should and should not.
2. What reason do you think is most important in deciding to let people live there?

UNIT 1 Review Test

I. Read the following sentences. Circle a, b, or c for the word or phrase that best completes each sentence.

1. There are five people on the _____ in my office.
   a. staff
   b. coworkers
   c. employees

2. To _____ their manager, each employee answered five questions.
   a. focus
   b. assess
   c. find out

3. I am very _____ about my new job. I like it a lot.
   a. concerned
   b. worried
   c. enthusiastic

4. It is _____ for you to finish this work by tomorrow. It must be done.
   a. enthusiastic
   b. essential
   c. hard

5. The new manager had a good _____. He liked the work and his staff.
   a. attitude
   b. team
   c. coworker

II. Read the exam questions below. For each sample answer, fill in the blanks using some of the words from the box.

1. According to the lecture, why is it important for a manager to talk to the employees?

employees	team	essential	enthusiastic
assess	problems	find out	

According to the lecture, it is important for a manager to talk to the employees so that they can work well together. A good manager knows the employees need to work together as a _____ and that a hard-working, _____ staff is
                              1.   2.
_____. A manager needs to _____ if he or she is doing a good
          3.   4.
job. By talking to the employees, the manager can find out what _____
                                                                          5.
people are having and how the work situation could be improved.

2. Describe what management assessment is.

content	staff	discuss	doing
answers	telling	vary	

Management assessment means _____ a manager good and bad points about
                                        1.

what she or he is _____. One way to do this is for the manager to give the
                          2.

_____ written questions. Each employee can write out _____ to
          3.   4.

the questions, then meet alone with the manager later to _____ the
                                                                    5.

assessment.

Now turn to page 121 to check your answers.

UNIT 2 Review Test

I. Read the following sentences. Use the word or phrase from the box that best completes each sentence. Be sure to use the correct form.

errors	influence	schedule
particular	available	reflect

1. I hope there is a computer _____ at the library. I need to write a letter.

2. There were some _____ in the computer program. It didn't work right.

3. In a computer program the instructions must be followed in a _____ order.

4. Language is like a mirror; it _____ how our society is changing.

5. More and more, computers are _____ how we talk.

II. Read the exam questions below. For each sample answer, fill in the blanks using some of the words from the box.

   1. Describe what the speaker feels is the relationship between computer use and how we talk. Use at least two examples from the lecture to support your answer.

off-line	on-line	computers	talk
access	interface	schedules	

The speaker believes that _____ have changed the way some people
                                                1.

_____. Here are two examples. First, someone might say, "Let's take this
         2.

discussion _____" to mean "Let's stop talking about this now." Someone
                    3.

might also say, "Let's try to _____ our _____ so we can have
                                         4.   5.

lunch together next week" to mean "Let's try to fit our schedules together so that we can

have lunch."

2. Explain what the expression "get with the program" means.

| reflect | instructions | supposed | correctly |
| program | followed | pay attention | |

"Get with the program" means to understand and follow what you are _____
1.
to be doing. In computer talk a _____ is a set of _____ that are
2. 3.
in a particular order. The program must be _____ to work _____.
4. 5.
If I tell you to "get with the program," I want you to do what we need to do.

Now turn to page 121 to check your answers.

UNIT 3 Review Test

I. Read the following sentences. Use the word or phrase from the box that best completes each sentence. Be sure to use the correct form.

develop	symptom	react	treat
theory	characteristic	classify	

1. One _____ of a phobia is extreme fear.

2. When the boy saw the dog, he _____ by crying.

3. Phobias are _____ by the thing that is feared.

4. To _____ the woman's phonophobia, the doctor used a toy telephone.

5. The little boy _____ hydrophobia after falling into a river.

II. Read the exam questions below. For each sample answer, fill in the blanks using some of the words from the box.

1. Explain the three characteristics of a phobia.

control	Greek	strong	long
treat	reasonable	fear	

There are three characteristics of a phobia. First, it is not a _____ reaction. It
                                                                      1.

is a reaction that is too _____ for the situation. Second, a phobia usually lasts
                          2.

for a _____ time, maybe for years. Finally, it is a _____ that is
       3.   4.

too strong to _____.
               5.

2. Describe the two main theories of why people have phobias.

| watching | deeper | symptom | strong |
| afraid | learned | control | treated |

There are two main theories about why people have phobias. The first is that a phobia is

_____. This means someone has a bad experience and becomes afraid, or
    1.

becomes afraid by _____ someone else. The second theory is that a phobia
                          2.

is only a _____ of a _____ problem. That is, when the person
                   3.   4.

acts _____, the real problem is not the phobia, but something else.
           5.

Now turn to page 122 to check your answers.

UNIT 4 Review Test

I. Circle a, b, or c for the word or phrase that best completes each sentence.

1. In the folktale "A Dinner of Smells" the restaurant owner was very _____ that the poor man smelled his food without paying for it.
  a. happy
  b. upset
  c. foolish

2. To _____ the poor man, the judge said he must pay the rich man.
  a. upset
  b. punish
  c. solve

3. In the folktale "A Dinner of Smells" the Effendi said that the poor man was his _____ brother.
  a. elder
  b. poorer
  c. wiser

4. The Effendi _____ the problem by shaking a bag of money.
  a. punished
  b. decided
  c. solved

5. After the Effendi shook the bag in "A Dinner of Smells," he said the _____ was paid.
  a. problem
  b. judge
  c. debt

II. Read the exam questions below. For each sample answer, fill in the blanks using some of the words from the box.

1. Describe why the poor man in the folktale "A Dinner of Smells" went to visit the Effendi.

pay	problem	coins	smell
court	judge	jingle	

The poor man went to visit the Effendi because he had a _____. The day
                                                          1.

before he had stopped to _____ some food in front of a restaurant. The
                                      2.

restaurant owner told him he had to _____ for the smells he took. The poor
                                        3.

man had to go to the _____ where the _____ would decide
                            4.   5.

how to punish him. The poor man wanted the Effendi to help him.

2. Explain what the Effendi teaches us in this story.

fair	solved	coins	foolish
power	angry	jingled	

The Effendi teaches us that people with power can be very _____ and unfair
                                                                    1.
sometimes. When the judge told the poor man he must pay the rich man, the Effendi

decided he would pay in a way that was _____ . He _____ a bag
                                            2.   3.
of _____ . The poor man ate only a smell, and the rich man was paid with
        4.
only a sound. The problem was _____ . The Effendi showed the judge and
                                    5.
the rich man that they should not use their power unfairly.

Now turn to page 122 to check your answers.

UNIT 5 Review Test

I. Read the following sentences. Use the word or phrase from the box that best completes each sentence. Be sure to use the correct form.

estimated	deal with	frustrated	average
concentrate	tune in	inherited	

1. Dr. Levinson says to think of our brains as TV sets and the parts of our brains that

_____ signals as computer chips.

2. That boy and his father both have trouble writing. Maybe the boy _____ the problem from his father.

3. Some children have trouble _____ in class. They listen to cars and birds, but they do not pay attention to the teacher.

4. It is _____ that one out of ten school children has dyslexia.

5. The girl started crying at school. She was _____ because she tried and tried to read, but she couldn't.

II. Read the exam questions below. For each sample answer, fill in the blanks using some of the words from the box.

1. Explain what dyslexia is. Include at least three examples of the kinds of problems children with dyslexia have.

range	understand	right	mathematics
average	drift	remembering	

Children with dyslexia have learning difficulties. There is a wide _____ of
1.

problems. Some children have problems reading. For example, they may be able to read

a sentence but not _____ what it means. Some have difficulty with
2.

directions; they cannot tell left from _____. Some have trouble with
3.

_____; they can't do simple number problems. There are other children who
4.

forget many things; some even have trouble _____ how to spell their own
5.

names.

2. Briefly explain Dr. Levinson's theory about why people have dyslexia.

brain	information	difficulty	TVs
drifts	reading	computer chips	

Dr. Levinson believes dyslexia is caused by the parts in the _____ that
1.
receive information not working correctly. He tells us to think of these parts as computer

chips that receive _____ about what we hear, touch, smell, and feel. He tells
2.

us to think of our brains as large _____ with many channels. The computer
3.

chips help us tune in each channel. If the brain can't tune in the signal of the information,

the signal _____ and the person has problems. The drifting can cause many
4.

types of problems, such as problems with _____.
5.

Now turn to page 123 to check your answers.

UNIT 6 Review Test

I. Read the following sentences. Use the word or phrase from the box that best completes each sentence. Be sure to use the correct form.

destroy	chant	tribes	balance
upset	heal	transfer	

1. The Navajo people are one of many _____ in North America.

2. According to the Navajos, if someone upsets the _____ in the world, the person becomes sick.

3. A medicine man is called to _____ the person.

4. The medicine man _____ the healing energy of the sand painting to the patient.

5. After the ceremony is finished, the sand painting is _____.

II. Read the exam questions below. For each sample answer, fill in the blanks using some of the words in the box.

1. Explain why a sand painting is made and who makes it.

decides	upsets	visits	symbol
chant	patient	heal	

A sand painting is made by a medicine man to heal someone. Navajos believe a person

becomes sick because he or she _____ the balance in the world. Making the
                                        1.

sand painting brings balance again and heals the _____. First, the medicine
                                                          2.

man _____ the patient and _____ what the problem is. Then he
          3.   4.

chooses the right sand painting and _____ to use.
                                              5.

2. Describe the process of making a sand painting.

colors	represent	sung over	transfer
throws	carry away	balance	

After the medicine man visits the sick person and decides which sand painting to make,

he slowly creates it using five main colors. The _____ have special meanings;
1.

for example, they _____ seasons and directions. After the sand painting is
2.

finished, the patient is _____. The patient sits in the middle of the sand
3.

painting and the medicine man sings and chants. Afterwards, the painting is destroyed.

The medicine man takes the sand outside and _____ it into the air to
4.

_____ the sickness.
5.

Now turn to page 123 to check your answers.

UNIT 7 Review Test

I. Read the following sentences. Use the word or phrase from the box that best completes each sentence. Be sure to use the correct form.

series	areas	compress	vibrate
continuous	crowded together	stored	

1. A sound wave has three _____ of pressure: high, low, and neutral.

2. When you strike a tuning fork, the prongs _____.

3. A sound wave is made up of a _____ of compressions and rarefactions.

4. In analog recording, the sound is recorded as a _____ stream of magnetism.

5. The main difference between analog and digital recording is how the sound is

_____.

II. Read the exam questions below. For each sample answer, fill in the blanks using some of the words from the box.

1. Explain what a sound is and what happens when a sound is made.

series	strike	creates	rarefactions
push	compressions	vibrate	

A sound is a series of air pressure changes. In a sound wave there are areas of high

pressure called _____ and areas of low pressure called _____.
　　　　　　　　　　　　　　1.　　　　　　　　　　　　　　　　　　　　　　　　　2.

In a compression, the molecules of air are crowded together. They _____
　　　　　　　　　　　　　　　　　　　　　　　　　　　　　　　　　　　　　　3.

against the next layer of air and a wave of compression spreads out. In a rarefaction, the

molecules spread apart and get thin. This _____ an empty space for other
　　　　　　　　　　　　　　　　　　　　　　4.

molecules to fill. The complete _____ of compressions and rarefactions is a
　　　　　　　　　　　　　　　　　5.

sound wave.

2. Compare analog and digital recording.

pattern	stored	bits	picture
treat	strike	continuous	

The two main ways of recording are analog and digital. The main difference is how the sound is _____. In analog recording, the sound is stored on tape as a
1.
representation or _____ of the sound. The magnetic _____ on
2.   3.
the tape is a copy of the sound. There is a continuous stream of magnetism. In digital recording, the sound is recorded and stored electronically as _____ of
4.
information. It is not stored as _____ information. When it is played back,
5.
it is put back together as continuous, however.

Now turn to page 124 to check your answers.

UNIT 8 Review Test

I. Read the following sentences. Circle a, b, or c for the word that best completes each sentence.

1. It is easier to grow food if the soil is
   _____.
   a. spreading
   b. packed down
   c. fertile

2. If trees are not replanted, rain and wind can cause the soil to _____.
   a. spread
   b. erode
   c. dry

3. As animals _____, they pack down the soil.
   a. graze
   b. rest
   c. grow

4. If the soil is packed down, it cannot hold _____ very well.
   a. moisture
   b. animals
   c. fertilizer

5. If there are fewer plants, the moisture _____ more quickly.
   a. erodes
   b. evaporates
   c. replants

II. Read the exam questions below. For each sample answer, fill in the blanks using some of the words from the box.

1. Describe what a desert region is like.

evaporates	dry	moisture	spread
fertilizer	soil	productive	

A desert region is very _____, with only a few plants and animals. Because
                              1.
there are few plants, it is difficult for the _____ to hold _____.
                                              2.   3.

In addition, the moisture _____ quickly. As a result, the land is not very
                          4.

_____; it is not fertile enough to grow food.
        5.

2. Give three reasons why topsoil is eroding and deserts are increasing.

overcutting	replanted	moisture	productive
fertilizer	pack down	spreading	

There are three main reasons why topsoil is eroding and deserts are _____.
                                                                                1.
First, 35 percent of erosion is caused by animals overgrazing. When the animals eat too

many plants, there is nothing to hold the soil. In addition, the animals _____
                                                                              2.
the soil, making it difficult for the soil to hold moisture. Second, 30 percent of erosion is

caused by the _____ of trees. Too many trees are cut down and not enough
                  3.
are _____. Third, 28 percent of erosion is caused by poor methods of
       4.
farming, such as using too much _____ or not letting the soil rest.
                                    5.

Now turn to page 124 to check your answers.

UNIT 9 Review Test

I. Read the following sentences. Circle a, b, or c for the word or phrase that best completes each sentence.

1. Photojournalists take pictures of _____ as they happen.
   a. people
   b. pyramids
   c. events

2. Photojournalists _____ some ethical questions because of the technology now available.
   a. face
   b. are based on
   c. alter

3. Electronic imaging can be used to _____ photographs.
   a. prove
   b. alter
   c. lie

4. Special _____ is no longer as important as the right computer system.
   a. proof
   b. worth
   c. training

5. Nowadays, can we still use a photograph to _____ something?
   a. prove
   b. face
   c. alter

II. Read the exam questions below. For each sample answer, fill in the blanks using some of the words from the box.

1. Explain how electronic imaging is used with photography.

difficult	prove	basic	manipulated
computer	truth	figure out	

Electronic imaging is a _____ technique used to change photographs. A
                              1.

photograph can be changed in _____ ways, and it is very _____
                                  2.   3.

to tell that the photograph has been altered. People and objects can be _____.
                                                                              4.

For example, a smile can be changed or a person moved. Because it is almost impossible

to tell a photograph has been changed, it's also difficult to _____ it.
                                                                    5.

2. Describe one ethical problem photojournalists have nowadays.

| events | alter | basic | based on |
| rules | truth | faced | |

Photojournalists are _____ with the problem of deciding if they should use a
1.
technology that is available. With electronic imaging they can _____
2.
photographs to get just the pictures they want. If they decide to use it, they must decide

what the _____ are. Expressions such as "Photos don't lie" are
3.

_____ the belief that photographs tell the truth. Most people still expect
4.

photojournalists to show us _____ as they really happen.
5.

Now turn to page 125 to check your answers.

UNIT 10 Review Test

I. Read the following sentences. Use the word or phrase from the box that best completes each sentence. Be sure to use the correct form.

inject	immune system	swelling	immunity
sensitive	confused	slightly	

1. During an anaphylactic reaction, someone can become very _____.

2. A normal reaction to a bee sting is pain, _____, and redness.

3. People who are allergic to bees are very _____ to bee venom.

4. A doctor _____ bee venom under the skin to test for an allergy.

5. Allergy shots are given to increase someone's _____.

II. Read the exam questions below. For each sample answer, fill in the blanks using some of the words from the box.

1. Describe an allergic reaction to a bee sting. Include at least three changes that occur in the body.

medicine	immune system	drops	antibodies
inject	pain	breathe	

An allergic reaction to a bee sting means that someone's body overreacts. The

_____ sends out _____ to protect the person, but the reaction is
     1.   2.

too strong. This very strong reaction, known as an anaphylactic reaction, affects the

whole body. There is pain and swelling all over the body. The legs, arms, and face can

turn red. It can be difficult to _____. The person becomes weak and
                                        3.

confused. The blood pressure _____. The person can die if he or she is not
                                      4.

given _____.
      5.

2. Explain how and why shots are given to someone allergic to bees.

more	slightly	sensitive	less
antibodies	increase	allergic	

Allergy shots are given to make an allergic person _____ sensitive to bee
                                                        1.

venom. The goal is to _____ immunity so that the person will not overreact
                          2.

if he or she is stung. In the allergy shots, the doctor uses a small amount of bee venom.

The doctor uses _____ more each visit. This helps the person slowly build
                     3.

immunity. Gradually, the person becomes less _____ to the venom. If the
                                                  4.

person gets stung, there will not be an _____ reaction.
                                            5.

Now turn to page 125 to check your answers.

UNIT 11 Review Test

I. Read the following sentences. Use the word or phrase from the box that best completes each sentence. Be sure to use the correct form.

affordable	accelerated	access	transmission
passive	enriched	unique	

1. Some say recorded music has _____ the spread of music around the world.

2. Musicians can combine different types of music to create something new and

   _____, something never heard before.

3. Because sound equipment is now _____, many people can hear recorded music at home.

4. Some people have become _____ because of recorded music. They hear it, but don't really listen to it.

5. People in many places now have _____ to music they couldn't hear before recorded music was so popular.

II. Read the exam questions below. For each sample answer, fill in the blanks using some of the words from the box.

1. What are the main advantages and disadvantages of recorded music?

rely on	enriched	local	hear
amateur	create	transmission	

The main advantage of recorded music is that people have access to music they would

not _____ otherwise. This has _____ their lives. The main
   　　　1.　　　　　　　　　　　　　　　　　2.

disadvantage is that there are fewer _____ musicians. Instead, most people
   　　　　　　　　　　　　　　　3.

_____ professionals to _____ the music they listen to.
   4.　　　　　　　　　　　　5.

2. Explain what World Music is. Give at least two examples.

rely on	recorded music	traditional	transmission
create	unique	South African	

World Music is an international style of music. It has developed because of the

accelerated _____ of musical styles made possible by _____.
                     1.   2.

World Music combines modern and _____ forms of music in
                                                             3.

_____ ways. Paul Simon's *Graceland,* made with _____
          4.   5.

musicians, and *A World Out of Time,* recorded in Madagascar by two American musicians,

are two of the many examples of World Music available today.

Now turn to page 126 to check your answers.

UNIT 12 Review Test

I. Read the following sentences. Circle a, b, or c for the word that best completes each sentence.

1. In a natural disaster, _____ is often destroyed.
   a. community
   b. mudflows
   c. property

2. The town estimated it needed $20 million to _____ from the storm.
   a. control
   b. recover
   c. erupt

3. One goal of a general plan is to _____ the amount of damage that can occur from a natural hazard.
   a. control
   b. recover
   c. rebuild

4. After a natural disaster such as a big earthquake, it can take a long time for a _____ to return to normal life.
   a. cooperation
   b. community
   c. destruction

5. More than 25,000 people were killed at Nevado del Ruiz when mudflows quickly _____ through the towns.
   a. swept
   b. controlled
   c. recovered

II. Read the exam questions below. For each sample answer, fill in the blanks using some of the words from the box.

1. What is the difference between a natural hazard and a natural disaster?

recover	natural hazards	property	natural disaster
community	control	cooperation	

There are things that happen in nature that can be dangerous to us. Hurricanes,

earthquakes, fires, flooding, and volcanic eruptions are examples of what are called

_____. In contrast, a _____ is when a lot of destruction occurs
    1.   2.

as the result of a natural hazard. For example, people are killed or hurt and

_____ is destroyed. It usually takes a lot of time and money to
    3.

_____. We cannot _____ a natural hazard, but we can plan ways
    4.   5.

to have fewer problems if one occurs.

2. Explain what happened in Nevado del Ruiz in 1985. What lesson was learned there?

erupted	cooperation	government	mudflows
community	recover	hazard	

In 1985, Nevado del Ruiz in Colombia _____. It was a small eruption, but it
                                              1.
melted snow and ice at the top of the volcano. This water joined water in the ground and

caused _____. The mudflows swept through the towns killing 25,000 people.
          2.
The lesson was that a good general plan is needed. _____ between scientists,
                                                          3.
the _____, and the people is necessary. Everyone in the _____
       4.   5.
needs to understand what to do before, during, and after a natural hazard happens to

keep it from becoming a disaster.

Now turn to page 126 to check your answers.

UNIT 1

VOCABULARY PREVIEW

2. essential **3.** content **4.** style **5.** staff **6.** assess
7. varied **8.** manager **9.** coworkers **10.** enthusiastic

LISTENING TO THE LECTURE

First Listening: Main Ideas

PART 1
1. b
2. c
PART 2
1. c
2. b

Second Listening: Facts and Details

PART 1
1. F
2. F
3. F
4. T
PART 2
1. F
2. T
3. T
4. T

UNIT 1 Review Test

I.

1. a **2.** b **3.** c **4.** b **5.** a

II.

QUESTION 1
1. team
2. enthusiastic
3. essential
4. find out
5. problems

QUESTION 2
1. telling
2. doing
3. staff
4. answers
5. discuss

UNIT 2

VOCABULARY PREVIEW

2. d **3.** f **4.** j **5.** i **6.** h **7.** a **8.** c **9.** b **10.** e

LISTENING TO THE LECTURE

First Listening: Main Ideas

PART 1
1. b
2. c
PART 2
1. c
2. a

Second Listening: Facts and Details

PART 1
1. F
2. F
3. F
4. T
PART 2
1. T
2. T
3. F
4. F

UNIT 2 Review Test

I.

1. available **2.** errors **3.** particular **4.** reflects
5. influencing

II.

QUESTION 1
1. computers
2. talk
3. off-line
4. interface
5. schedules

QUESTION 2
1. supposed
2. program
3. instructions
4. followed
5. correctly

UNIT 3

VOCABULARY PREVIEW
2. h **3.** a **4.** b **5.** j **6.** g **7.** d **8.** e **9.** f **10.** i

LISTENING TO THE LECTURE

First Listening: **Main Ideas**	**Second Listening:** **Facts and Details**
PART 1	PART 1
1. c	**1.** T
2. a	**2.** F
PART 2	**3.** F
1. b	**4.** T
2. a	PART 2
	1. T
	2. F
	3. T
	4. F

UNIT 3 Review Test

I.

1. characteristic **2.** reacted **3.** classified **4.** treat
5. developed

II.

QUESTION 1
1. reasonable
2. strong
3. long
4. fear
5. control

QUESTION 2
1. learned
2. watching
3. symptom
4. deeper
5. afraid

UNIT 4

VOCABULARY PREVIEW
2. i **3.** j **4.** b **5.** c **6.** g **7.** e **8.** a **9.** d **10.** f

LISTENING TO THE LECTURE

First Listening: **Main Ideas**	**Second Listening:** **Facts and Details**
PART 1	PART 1
1. b	**1.** F
2. c	**2.** T
PART 2	**3.** F
1. a	**4.** T
2. b	PART 2
	1. T
	2. F
	3. F
	4. T

UNIT 4 Review Test

I.

1. b **2.** b **3.** a **4.** c **5.** c

II.

QUESTION 1
1. problem
2. smell
3. pay
4. court
5. judge

QUESTION 2
1. foolish
2. fair
3. jingled
4. coins
5. solved

UNIT 5

VOCABULARY PREVIEW
2. frustrated **3.** estimate **4.** average **5.** consider
6. to deal with **7.** tune **8.** concentrate **9.** drifts
10. inherited

LISTENING TO THE LECTURE

First Listening: Main Ideas	Second Listening: Facts and Details
PART 1	PART 1
1. b	**1.** T
2. a	**2.** F
PART 2	**3.** T
1. b	**4.** F
2. c	PART 2
	1. T
	2. T
	3. F
	4. T

UNIT 5 Review Test

I.

1. tune in **2.** inherited **3.** concentrating **4.** estimated
5. frustrated

II.

QUESTION 1
1. range
2. understand
3. right
4. mathematics
5. remembering

QUESTION 2
1. brain
2. information
3. TVs
4. drifts
5. reading

UNIT 6

VOCABULARY PREVIEW
2. f **3.** i **4.** e **5.** h **6.** g **7.** c **8.** b **9.** d **10.** a

LISTENING TO THE LECTURE

First Listening: Main Ideas	Second Listening: Facts and Details
PART 1	PART 1
1. a	**1.** F
2. c	**2.** T
PART 2	**3.** T
1. c	**4.** F
2. a	PART 2
	1. F
	2. T
	3. F
	4. T

UNIT 6 Review Test

I.

1. tribes **2.** balance **3.** heal **4.** transfers **5.** destroyed

II.

QUESTION 1
1. upsets
2. patient
3. visits
4. decides
5. chant

QUESTION 2
1. colors
2. represent
3. sung over
4. throws
5. carry away

UNIT 7

VOCABULARY PREVIEW
2. strike **3.** area **4.** original **5.** series **6.** spread out
7. store **8.** create **9.** vibrates **10.** patterns

LISTENING TO THE LECTURE

First Listening: Main Ideas	Second Listening: Facts and Details
PART 1	PART 1
1. a	**1.** F
2. c	**2.** T
PART 2	**3.** T
1. c	**4.** F
2. b	PART 2
	1. T
	2. T
	3. F
	4. T

UNIT 7 Review Test

I.
1. areas **2.** vibrate **3.** series **4.** continuous **5.** stored

II.
QUESTION 1
1. compressions
2. rarefactions
3. push
4. creates
5. series

QUESTION 2
1. stored
2. picture
3. pattern
4. bits
5. continuous

UNIT 8

VOCABULARY PREVIEW
2. d **3.** b **4.** h **5.** f **6.** i **7.** j **8.** c **9.** g **10.** a

LISTENING TO THE LECTURE

First Listening: Main Ideas	Second Listening: Facts and Details
PART 1	PART 1
1. c	**1.** T
2. b	**2.** T
PART 2	**3.** F
1. b	**4.** T
2. c	PART 2
	1. F
	2. F
	3. T
	4. T

UNIT 8 Review Test

I.
1. c **2.** b **3.** a **4.** a **5.** b

II.
QUESTION 1
1. dry
2. soil
3. moisture
4. evaporates
5. productive

QUESTION 2
1. spreading
2. pack down
3. overcutting
4. replanted
5. fertilizer

UNIT 9

VOCABULARY PREVIEW

2. ethical **3.** event **4.** worth **5.** based on **6.** prove
7. manipulate **8.** alter **9.** basic **10.** training

LISTENING TO THE LECTURE

First Listening: Main Ideas	Second Listening: Facts and Details
PART 1	PART 1
1. b	**1.** T
2. a	**2.** F
PART 2	**3.** F
1. c	**4.** T
2. b	PART 2
	1. T
	2. F
	3. T
	4. F

UNIT 9 Review Test

I.

1. c **2.** a **3.** b **4.** c **5.** a

II.

QUESTION 1
1. computer
2. basic
3. difficult
4. manipulated
5. prove

QUESTION 2
1. faced
2. alter
3. rules
4. based on
5. events

UNIT 10

VOCABULARY PREVIEW

2. slightly **3.** venom **4.** confused **5.** swelling
6. antibodies **7.** immunity **8.** sensitive **9.** sting
10. inject

LISTENING TO THE LECTURE

First Listening: Main Ideas	Second Listening: Facts and Details
PART 1	PART 1
1. c	**1.** T
2. b	**2.** T
PART 2	**3.** F
1. a	**4.** F
2. c	PART 2
	1. T
	2. F
	3. F
	4. F

UNIT 10 Review Test

I.

1. confused **2.** swelling **3.** sensitive **4.** injects
5. immunity

II.

QUESTION 1
1. immune system
2. antibodies
3. breathe
4. drops
5. medicine

QUESTION 2
1. less
2. increase
3. slightly
4. sensitive
5. allergic

UNIT 11

VOCABULARY PREVIEW
2. rely on   **3.** affordable   **4.** passive   **5.** unique
6. amateur   **7.** accelerated   **8.** access   **9.** enriched
10. local

LISTENING TO THE LECTURE

First Listening: Main Ideas	Second Listening: Facts and Details
PART 1	PART 1
1. c	**1.** F
2. b	**2.** F
PART 2	**3.** T
1. a	**4.** T
2. b	PART 2
	1. F
	2. T
	3. F
	4. T

UNIT 11 Review Test

I.
1. accelerated   **2.** unique   **3.** affordable   **4.** passive
5. access

II.
QUESTION 1
1. hear
2. enriched
3. amateur
4. rely on
5. create

QUESTION 2
1. transmission
2. recorded music
3. traditional
4. unique
5. South African

UNIT 12

VOCABULARY PREVIEW
2. recover   **3.** erupted   **4.** control   **5.** disaster   **6.** swept
7. cooperation   **8.** property   **9.** community
10. destruction

LISTENING TO THE LECTURE

First Listening: Main Ideas	Second Listening: Facts and Details
PART 1	PART 1
1. c	**1.** F
2. b	**2.** T
PART 2	**3.** F
1. a	**4.** F
2. b	PART 2
	1. T
	2. F
	3. F
	4. T

UNIT 12 Review Test

I.
1. c   **2.** b   **3.** a   **4.** b   **5.** a

II.
QUESTION 1
1. natural hazards
2. natural disaster
3. property
4. recover
5. control

QUESTION 2
1. erupted
2. mudflows
3. cooperation
4. government
5. community

UNIT 1 A Good Manager

Narrator: In this lecture, the speaker discusses managers and how to assess managers. In Part 1, you will hear about a situation between a manager, Mr. Thomas, and an employee, Linda Jones.

PART 1

Hello everyone. Today our lecture is going to be about business management. Specifically, I'm going to talk a little about managers, what makes someone a good **manager.** OK? Now first, I'll describe a work **situation** for you . . . and then I'll explain one important management **technique.**

OK, then let's begin. First off, let's consider an office situation in the United States. Let's say that we have a company called the, um, ABC company, and there's a new manager, named Mr. Thomas, who has just started working at one office of this company. OK? A new manager on the job. One day, an **employee**—let's call her Linda Jones—went to talk to Mr. Thomas. She was having some problems with her work, and she wanted to talk to her manager about these problems. Her problem was this: Mr. Thomas **organized** the office work in a new and different way, and it was becoming more difficult for her to do her job. And she also felt that Mr. Thomas wasn't very clear about what she was supposed to do. She wanted to know more clearly, "What am I supposed to do? What do you expect of me?"

All right, so let's think about this. Ms. Jones goes to Mr. Thomas to talk about the work situation. Now for most employees, asking a manager questions like this is hard. In this case, it was hard for Linda to talk to Mr. Thomas, but she felt she had to do it. She had worked in the office for five years, and, of course, she didn't want to lose her job because she couldn't get her job done. She also didn't want to quit her job because of the problems. She just wasn't **content** the way the office was being **run,** and she needed to talk about it.

Now let's think about the manager's position. In this case, Mr. Thomas was very surprised when he first heard that she was having problems. He was surprised . . . and **irritated.** There was too much work to do, right? He didn't really want to deal with

a **personal** problem. He didn't think this was a work problem, and he felt he was too busy to think about problems people might be having.

But later, Mr. Thomas thought about what Linda said. He thought, "Aha, this *is* a work problem." And he realized he needed to find out from the other people in the office, from her **coworkers,** if they were having problems, too.

All right, let's pause for a moment and look at what Mr. Thomas, as the manager, had to consider. First of all, a good manager understands that a hardworking, **enthusiastic staff** is very important. In fact, we could say it is **essential** . . . absolutely essential. All of the employees need to work together. They need to work as a team to make the company successful. And, of course, part of feeling like a team is feeling that what each person does and says is important.

Well, as in most work situations, we have a problem here with communication. That is, most managers do not want to hear people **complain,** and most employees are afraid to come right out and say what they feel. They usually won't say what they like or don't like. They may complain to each other during lunch or after work, but they do not complain directly to the manager.

It is important, however, for a manager to find out if he or she is doing a good job. One way to do this is to give employees a chance to talk. Employees need an **opportunity** to say what is wrong, what they don't like about the work situation, and what they would change to make their work better. However, most employees are afraid to say what they feel. This is why a manager needs to figure out a safe way for people to talk. By safe, I mean a way to talk where people aren't afraid something will happen to them if they tell the **truth.** It has to be safe, or else people just won't say what they're thinking.

Narrator: Stop the tape and answer the questions for Part 1.

Narrator: Now let's continue with Part 2. In this part of the lecture, you will hear about ways of assessing a manager. You will also be looking at a manager assessment form. You can prepare by reading over the form on page 5.

PART 2

Now let's look a little bit more closely at what a manager can do. According to some management **consultants,** a manager needs to give employees a clear way of assessing him or her. By assessing I mean a way of telling the manager good and bad points about what he or she is doing. Right? Tell me my good and bad points—that's an **assessment.** One way the manager can have employees do this is to give them questions to answer in writing. OK? Not asking them orally, but giving them a chance to write their assessments. Then the manager can meet with each employee and discuss what he or she wrote.

Now asking for an assessment is not so easy. It is important for the manager to ask the right kind of questions. If the manager asks direct questions like "Do you like me?" or "Do you like the way I ask you to do things?" the employee probably won't tell the truth. I mean, would you tell the truth if you were asked this kind of question? These questions are just too direct and, um, just too personal: They focus too much on personal feelings.

On the other hand, if the manager asks questions like "How would it be easier for you to do your job?" or "How could things be done differently?" it's easier for an employee to answer **honestly.** Do you see the difference here? It is easier to answer because the question **focuses** on the work itself. The question doesn't focus on the employee's feelings about the manager. It shows the employee the question is being asked in order to make it easier to get the job done well.

OK, now I'd like you to have a look at a sample assessment form. Please look at the figure on page 5 for a minute. This shows some questions from a management assessment form. Follow along as I go over the questions. Ready?

Number 1, "Do I give clear directions?"

Number 2, "Do you need help from coworkers to understand what I want?" Number 3, "Do I change my mind too often about what I want you to do?" Number 4, "Do I listen to new ideas and ways of doing things?" Number 5, "Do you come to me when you need help?" And Number 6, "Do I tell you when you have done a good job?"

OK, so think about these questions. What are they about? What's the purpose of these questions? I think . . . I think we have to notice that these questions show certain **attitudes** about how an American manager should act . . . . They show us what an American manager is supposed to do in his or her job. These questions also tell us—and this is very interesting—they show us something about the **relationship** between manager and employees . . . what the relationship between the employees and the manager is **expected** to be. Management assessment today is based on the idea of solving problems and communicating so that everyone will feel they are part of a team. Let me repeat that because this is a key point: Management assessment is based on the idea of solving problems and **communicating** so that everyone will feel they are part of a team.

OK, now please note that this is an American model or idea for management assessment. Of course, business styles and management **styles vary** from culture to culture. This particular style of management assessment may not work in every culture. For any country or culture, it is important to think about how work is done and how **decisions** are made. And it's very important to consider how people communicate. All right? Well, that's all for today.

Narrator: Stop the tape and answer the questions for Part 2.

UNIT 2 Computers and How We Talk

Narrator: In this lecture, the speaker will give four examples of how computer language is used in everyday situations. Listen for the examples, and think about what they mean.

PART 1

Hello. I think we can begin now if you're ready. . . . Um, today I want to talk to you about computers . . . about the **impact** of computers on how we talk . . . on the ways we talk. Now of course we all know that computers have changed our lives in many ways. Stop and think for a minute about how we use computers in our everyday life. It's hard to think of *any*thing we do that hasn't been changed by computers. For example, computers

allow us to get money **directly** from our **bank accounts** at cash machines. At hospitals, computers help doctors understand what is wrong with patients. We can use computers to help us decide which color to paint our houses, which **hair styles** to have, or which dresses or suits would look good on us . . . lots of professional and personal uses. Computers are simply a part of our lives, and, I think it is safe to say, they will **continue** to be. What I'd like to look at today is how the use of computers has had an impact on our language—how computers have changed the expressions we say, the words we use.

First, um, let me give you some examples. These are examples from English that I'd like you to think about. The first example is this. Someone at an office says, "We'd like to have the **project** on-line by next Monday." . . . "We'd like to have the project on-line by next Monday." In computer talk "on-line" means started or working—part of the **system.** So this statement means that we'd like to have the project started and going by next Monday.

The second example is from a discussion or seminar. Someone might say, "Let's take this discussion **off-line** until tomorrow." . . . "Let's take this discussion off-line until tomorrow." To take a computer "off-line" means to **disconnect** it or take it out of the system. What do you think it means to take a discussion off-line? To take a discussion "off-line" means to stop talking about something. This example means "let's stop discussing this now and talk about it tomorrow."

The third example is: "I'll try to **interface** my plans with yours." . . . "I'll try to interface my plans with yours." To "interface," in computer talk, means to do something so that different computer parts or **software** can work together. So "I'll try to interface my plans with yours" means that "I'll try to change my plans to fit with yours." People still say, of course, "I'll try to change my plans to fit with yours." But now we might also start to hear people say, "I'll try to interface my plans with yours," or "Let's see if we can interface our **schedules** so that we can meet next week."

Let's try one more example. Our fourth example might take place at home. Someone says, "I just can't access where I left my car keys." . . . "I just can't access where I left my car keys." In computer talk to "access" something means to make

information **available.** If I can't access where I left my keys, I don't have this information available for me to use. What would be another way to say this? Of course, we could also say, "I can't remember where I put my keys."

Narrator: Stop the tape and answer the questions for Part 1.

Narrator: Now let's continue with Part 2. In this part of the lecture, the speaker gives one more example. Then the speaker asks, "Will computer language become more common in our everyday lives?" Think about this question as you listen.

PART 2

OK, with these examples here, I think you're getting the picture of how computer expressions are becoming part of our everyday language. Let me give you just one more example. Maybe you've heard this one several times before.

Let's **suppose** two people are working together. One person gets angry because the other person doesn't seem to understand what is going on. The first person yells, "Get with the **program!**" In computer talk a "program" is a group of instructions that are planned in a **particular** order. One instruction leads to another instruction. "To get with the program" means to pay attention—to follow what we're supposed to be doing.

Now let's think about what this means. Do computers affect our language and our thought? Will computer language become more common in our everyday lives? The answer, as you can guess, is probably yes. Of course, it is hard to tell what the **long-term** effect of computers on language will be. Some computer words and expressions will only be **jargon.** This means they may be popular only with people who work with computers, but never spread into **daily** use by other people.

But other words and expressions will be used more and more by people who do not work with computers. And, yes, these words will gradually become a more important part of the language of everyone. For example, consider the word *bug*. A computer bug is an **error** or problem. When it was first used . . . let's see . . . maybe back in the 1970s . . . it was just an industry word. By this I mean it was just used by people who worked with computers. But, of course, now the word *bug* is used more and more frequently by other people in their daily lives. Most speakers of English would probably understand the sentence "I think your plan has a lot of bugs in it" to mean that I think your plan has some problems or weak points. This to me is a clear example of a word making the change— the **transition**—from jargon to more regular usage. We will have to wait some more years to see if it truly becomes a part of the English language.

OK, well that is basically it. I want you to understand one key point here—that language is always changing. Language has been called a **mirror** of **society.** It is a mirror because it **reflects** the changes in our society, and the way our society is. And our society, our world, is changing because computers are being used more and more. So it's likely that computers will continue to **influence** us, including the way we talk and the words we use. All right, so let's stop there for today.

Narrator: Stop the tape and answer the questions for Part 2.

UNIT 3 Be Careful: Phobias

Narrator: In this lecture, you will hear about phobias. You'll hear a definition and three characteristics of a phobia. Then you'll hear some examples.

PART 1

OK, I think we can continue our discussion now. . . . We were talking before about some common psychological problems, problems of the mind. Today we're going to continue this discussion . . . and talk about one kind of psychological problem: a phobia. First, we'll talk about what a phobia is. I'll give you examples of a few phobias, and I think you'll be interested in this . . . and then I'll talk about some reasons . . . reasons why people have phobias.

Let's first look at what a phobia is. As you probably know, a phobia is really a fear. It is not a

normal fear, however; it is an **extreme** fear—a fear that someone *always* has. Now, we can note that there are three **characteristics** of a phobia . . . three characteristics. First, a phobia is not a **reasonable** reaction. By this I mean it is a very, very strong reaction, too strong for the situation. Second, it is . . . a phobia is . . . a reaction that someone **continues** to have for a long time. It can be for years or for an entire lifetime. Third, the reaction is too strong for a person to **control.** This means that even if the person tries not to be afraid, he or she cannot control the fear. OK, those are the three characteristics.

Now, let's think about some classifications. Phobias are **classified** by the thing that is feared . . . by the thing that the person fears. **Greek** or **Latin** names are used to describe what is feared. Here's an example: *hydro,* h-y-d-r-o, means water. Fear of water then is hydrophobia.

Here's another example: *hypno,* h-y-p-n-o, means sleep. So fear of sleep is hypnophobia. I wonder if any of you have these phobias. No? OK, well, now let's see if you can answer a couple of questions about phobias: First, *cyno,* c-y-n-o, means dog. What is a fear of dogs? Just write down your answer. And . . . second question, *phono,* p-h-o-n-o, means sound, or phone, as in telephone. What do you think phonophobia is? OK, got that? Here are the answers. A fear of dogs is cynophobia. And phonophobia is a fear of talking on the telephone.

Narrator: Stop the tape and answer the questions for Part 1.

Narrator: Now let's continue with Part 2. In this part of the lecture, the speaker will talk about what causes a phobia. There are two theories about the cause of phobias. Listen for the difference between these theories.

PART 2

Let's turn now to the causes of phobias. **Psychologists** are interested in how the human mind works, and so some psychologists have studied why people have phobias. There are two main **theories** about what **causes** phobias. One theory is that a phobia is learned. For example, let's say a girl gets bitten by a big dog when she is three years old. This is a terrible **experience** for her. I mean, just imagine how frightening that would be. From this experience, she learns to be very afraid of dogs. Every time she sees a dog, she feels afraid. She develops cynophobia.

There is another way she could learn to **develop** this phobia. She could also learn to have cynophobia by watching how other people **react** to dogs. Let's **imagine** that the girl's father is very afraid of dogs. Whenever the girl and her father are in a park and see a dog, the father gets very scared. The girl sees how her father reacts. The girl becomes very scared, too. The girl develops cynophobia. She learns it from someone else. OK, so the first theory is that a phobia is learned.

The other theory, the second theory, says that a phobia is only a sign or a **symptom** of another problem. This means that the phobia isn't the real problem. The real problem is something else, and it's usually a serious **emotional** problem. To use the example of cynophobia again, let's say there is a woman who acts very afraid of dogs. She has cynophobia. According to this theory, though, she actually has another problem. When she acts afraid of dogs, she is really showing her fear of something else. Let's say she is afraid of her father. Maybe her father was very strict when she was young . . . . He yelled at her a lot . . . . She was, and maybe she still is, afraid of him. Her fear of dogs is only a sign of her serious problem concerning her father. In other words, the phobia is a symptom of her deep problem with her father—at least, according to this theory.

OK, so let's think about these two theories. There is one main difference between them. The first theory says that the phobia is the problem itself. The second theory says that the phobia is a sign, just a sign of some other problem the person has. This difference is important because it affects how the phobia is **treated** . . . . If we know the cause, we can find the best treatment.

According to the first theory, if a phobia is learned, perhaps it can be *un*learned. A psychologist who believes this theory will try to teach someone to react differently when he or she sees a dog. A psychologist who believes the second theory will do something very different . . . will try a very different treatment. This psychologist may start by talking about the phobia. The doctor tries to

do more, though. The doctor's **goal** is to find out what the patient's deep emotional problem is. Then the doctor tries to help the patient with that problem. In other words, the doctor helps the patient find the deeper problem and how this deeper problem is related to the phobia.

OK, so I hope you understand this difference . . . between the two theories about what causes phobias. Are there any questions?

Narrator: Stop the tape and answer the questions for Part 2.

UNIT 4 A Lesson in Folktales

Narrator: In this lecture, you will hear a folktale called "A Dinner of Smells." Listen for the main actions in the story. What was the problem? How was it solved?

PART 1

Today we're going to start talking about folktales. As you know, every country has folktales. Today we're going to hear one folktale and talk about it a little bit. The fable I've chosen for today is a Uygur folktale. Uygurs, by the way, are a Chinese Muslim group. Now, this folktale is an Effendi Nasreddin tale called "A Dinner of Smells." Some of you may know these tales. The Effendi Nasreddin is well known throughout the Muslim world. Usually, he is just called the Effendi.

In this simple folktale, you're going to hear how the Effendi fights back against a restaurant owner he thinks is being **unfair.** OK, so here's the story.

One day, a poor man came to visit the Effendi. This man wanted the Effendi to help him. He said, "Nasreddin, I need your help. I don't know if you will help me. I am a poor man, a man with no money."

The Effendi looked at him kindly and answered, "I'll help you. Tell me what is wrong."

The poor man explained what was wrong. He said, "Yesterday I stopped in front of the door of a restaurant. The restaurant **belonged to** a rich man. I ate nothing. I only smelled the food. However, the owner came out and noticed me. He said that I was enjoying his food—and he wanted me to pay him for the food. Of course, I had no money with me to pay him, and then he became very angry. And he called the **judge.** The judge said I must go to the **court** today. He will tell me how I will be **punished.** Please, Nasreddin, can you help me? Can you say something to the judge?"

Nasreddin thought for a moment, and then he said, "Yes. I'll go to the court with you. Let's go." And they left together for the court. When the Effendi and the poor man got to the court, the rich man was already there waiting. Right away, this rich man began shouting angrily at the poor man. Then the judge started talking. "You see how angry he is?" the judge said. "You have filled yourself up on the smell of his restaurant. Yet, you have not even paid him. You must pay him right now!"

After the Effendi heard what the judge said, he stepped forward. He looked at the rich man. Then he said, "Oh, sir, do not be so **upset.** You will become **ill.** This poor man is my brother. My **elder** brother. He is a poor man, and he cannot pay you. So, I will pay you instead."

After he heard this, the rich man smiled, thinking about his payment. Then the Effendi took a bag of money from his **belt,** a bag of **copper coins.** He bent down next to the rich man and shook the bag. When he shook the bag, the coins **jingled** loudly. "Listen," he said to the rich man. "Do you hear this sound?"

"Of course I hear it, of course I hear it," shouted the rich man **impatiently.**

"Well, then," answered the Effendi, "the problem is **solved.** The **debt** is paid. My brother has smelled your food, and you have heard his money."

Afterwards, the Effendi Nasreddin took the arm of the poor man. They left the court together. The poor man was **saved.**

Narrator: Stop the tape and answer the questions for Part 1.

Narrator: Now let's continue with Part 2. In this part of the lecture, you will hear some of the things these folktales teach listeners. You will then hear the story again, along with a short analysis of the story.

PART 2

Now let's look at the story more closely. What does the Effendi teach us in this story? Many of the

Effendi tales are about the same or similar ideas. I'll list these for you. First, well, the first idea is that people who have power often use it unfairly. Second, the second idea in these tales is that people who are rich and **powerful** can also be **stupid** and **immoral.** And the third idea is that common, um, **common people,** poor people, can be very **wise.** Now let's listen to the story again and think about these three ideas—Who uses power unfairly? How is someone rich and powerful **foolish** here? And how does a common person, the Effendi, show he is wise? Listen.

One day, a poor man came to visit the Effendi because he wanted the Effendi to help him. He said, "Nasreddin, I need your help. I don't know if you can help me because I am just a poor man, a man with no money."

The Effendi answered quietly, "Calm down. I'll help you. Tell me what is wrong."

The poor man explained what was wrong. "Well, yesterday I stopped in front of the door of a restaurant, a restaurant that belonged to a rich man. I did not eat anything, I only smelled the food. However, the man, the owner, said that I must pay for the smell of the food. When I told him that I had no money with me to pay him, he became very angry and called the judge. The judge said I must go to the court today. I will be punished. Please, can you help me? Can you say something to the judge?"

"Yes," said the Effendi, "I'll go to the court with you. Let's go." And they left together for the court.

Now, here, in this first part of the story, you can see that the Effendi realizes that a powerful person is unfair. The restaurant owner is being unfair to a poor person.

So the story continues: When the Effendi and the poor man got to the court, the rich man was already there. The rich man began shouting angrily at the poor man. Then the judge started talking. "You see how angry he is?" the judge said. "You have filled yourself up on the smell of his restaurant. Yet, you have not even paid him. You must pay him right now!"

Here we can see that both the judge and restaurant owner are being stupid and immoral. They believe that powerful people can do whatever they wish.

And the story goes on: After the Effendi heard what the judge said, he stepped forward. He looked at the rich man and said, "Oh, sir, do not be so upset. You will become ill. This poor man is my brother. My elder brother. He is a poor man, and he cannot pay you. So, I will pay you instead."

Hearing this, the rich man smiled. Then the Effendi took a bag of money from his belt, a bag of copper coins. He bent down next to the rich man and shook the bag. When he shook the bag, the coins jingled. "Listen," he said to the rich man. "Do you hear this sound?"

"Of course I hear it, of course I hear it," shouted the rich man impatiently.

"Well, then," answered the Effendi, "the problem is solved. The debt is paid. My brother has smelled your food, and you have heard his money."

Afterwards, the Effendi Nasreddin took the arm of the poor man. They left the court together. The poor man was saved.

In the final part of the story, we can see that the Effendi, who is acting as a simple, common person, is actually very wise, and that wisdom—not power—solves the problem.

So, there so you can see the three ideas in this story. I said earlier that many of the Effendi tales are about these same ideas. In the next class we'll talk about some other tales.

Narrator: Stop the tape and answer the questions for Part 2.

UNIT 5   Learning Difficulties: Dyslexia

Narrator: In the first part of this lecture, the speaker describes problems that people with dyslexia have. Listen for what these problems are. The speaker also talks about the cause of dyslexia.

PART 1

Hello everyone. I think we can get started now. As we have studied in this class, there are many different learning problems people can have. Today I'd like to talk about one of them—dyslexia. In the first part of my talk, I'll briefly explain what dyslexia is, and give you some general background about it.

First, the word itself, *dyslexia,* d-y-s-l-e-x-i-a, is from Greek. It means **difficulty** with words and

language . . . difficulty with words, with using words. However, dyslexia is more than just a difficulty with language. It includes a number of learning difficulties, and it has a wide **range** of symptoms. Some people have difficulty learning to read and write. For example, a child may see p-o-t, but read it as t-o-p, or a child may be able to read all of the words in a sentence, but not understand what it means. These are both examples of problems with dyslexia.

There can be other related problems. Some people with dyslexia have difficulty with directions: They can't tell right from left easily, or they can't tell the **difference between up and down,** or top and bottom. Some people with dyslexia have difficulty learning to tell time, or to tie their shoes. These are kinds of problems with directions. Other people with dyslexia may be unable to **concentrate;** it is hard for them to **pay attention.** Do you know what I mean—they have difficulties with concentrating, with paying attention to what other people say? Other people with dyslexia often forget things, even how to spell their own names. OK, so these are related problems with learning and memory. In addition, about 60 percent of dyslexics, 60 percent of people with dyslexia, have difficulty with **basic** mathematics. They may have trouble adding even simple numbers. So, this is the range of problems that people with dyslexia might have.

Well, you might ask, "Is it common? Is dyslexia a common problem?" Unfortunately, the answer is yes. It is **estimated** that one out of ten school children has dyslexia—10 percent of all school children will have dyslexia. And dyslexia actually affects both boys and girls. For a long time, people thought of dyslexia as only a boys' problem, but now we know that it affects both girls and boys. However, it may only seem like more boys have it because more boys than girls are tested for it.

OK, so that's the size of the problem, but where, where does dyslexia come from? Dyslexia is believed to be **inherited.** For 85 percent of children with dyslexia, there is someone else in the family who also has it—usually the mother or the father.

As you can guess, children with dyslexia often have trouble at school. They are generally **smart,** though. On **standardized intelligence tests,** they usually have **average** or higher-than-average **scores.** Other people, sometimes even their teachers, however, usually don't **consider** them to be very smart. And dyslexics often don't feel very smart, either. They feel like there is something wrong with them. They know they can't learn the same way other kids at school can. They often don't know why, though, and they just blame themselves.

To sum up the main points I've made so far: First, **dyslexic** children have learning difficulties. They may have trouble learning certain skills such as speaking, reading, writing, mathematics, or telling time. Or they may have difficulty sitting still in school, paying attention, concentrating on the lesson. There are many different kinds of problems dyslexics can have. The reason, though, is the same. A dyslexic person's brain works differently from other people's. This is a key point, so I'll say it again. Their brains work differently from other people's.

Narrator: Stop the tape and answer the questions for Part 1.

Narrator: Now let's continue with Part 2. In this part of the lecture, the speaker further describes the problem of dyslexia. He compares the brain to a TV set. This comparison helps to explain how dyslexics read or listen differently from other people.

PART 2

In this part of the lecture, I'd like to talk about the work of Dr. Harold Levinson, a doctor who has studied dyslexia, has studied people with dyslexia for a long time. He has written an important book to help us understand what dyslexia is and how **to deal with** it.

Dr. Levinson is the **director** of the Dyslexic Treatment Center in Great Neck, New York. One book he has written is called the *Upside-Down Kids.* In this book, he talks about eight children who have problems in school. He calls the kids "upside-down" because their brains work differently from other people's.

To help us understand dyslexia, he tells us to think of our brains as TV sets, and to think of the parts in our brains that receive information as **computer chips.** Remember, this idea is that the brain is a TV set, and the parts in the brain that receive information are computer chips. Every day,

the computer chips receive information. Right? Every day, the information comes in as signals to the brain. The signals are about what we see, what we hear and touch, and what we feel both inside and outside our bodies. OK, information from our senses. The job of the computer chips is to **tune in** the signals to different **channels** in our brain. They try to tune in the signals just like your TV set at home does. If the computer chips aren't working right, they can't tune in the signals correctly. . . . The signals aren't clear. This means they can't tune in the correct channels. Instead, the signals **drift** around and become unclear. OK, so when a signal keeps drifting there is a problem. For example, if a child cannot tune in to the signals on a page when she reads, she has difficulty reading. If she cannot tune in signals from something she is hearing, she has difficulty hearing information correctly; the information may sound all **mixed up.**

Our brains, or our mental TV sets, have millions of channels, a lot more than you have on your TV set at home. Because there are millions of channels, there are many different problems children can have. Dr. Levinson believes these computer chips control more than just our **ability** to write, walk, read, and speak. They also control energy levels. This is why some children have difficulty sitting still. They also control our ability to concentrate, and to tell the difference between what is important and what is unimportant. For example, some children at school concentrate on the wrong things. As the teacher writes on the chalkboard, they concentrate on the sound of the **chalk,** or the movement of her hand. They don't, however, listen to the ideas that she is talking about.

It sounds like life is difficult for children with dyslexia, doesn't it? The good news is that Dr. Levinson believes that the brain can learn to fix the drifting. As a result, some children's problems disappear as they get older.

Dyslexia is a very interesting problem. But, of course, it is not a simple problem. Doctors, teachers, and **researchers** are now starting to understand dyslexia a little bit better, though. Dyslexic children have often felt **hopeless** and **frustrated** at school. They sometimes **give up** and **blame** themselves for not doing well in school. Dr. Levinson thinks schools need to change their **attitudes** toward children with dyslexia. He believes children with dyslexia need to be thought of as people who learn *differently,* not as people who can't or don't want to learn.

OK, well, I think that that's enough for today. We'll talk more about other learning problems in our next class.

Narrator: Stop the tape and answer the questions for Part 2.

UNIT 6 Sand Painting

Narrator: In this lecture, you will learn about sand painting, which is part of a healing ritual of the Navajo people. In the first part of the lecture, you will learn who makes sand paintings. You will also learn about the steps in selecting and making a sand painting.

PART 1

This week I plan to talk about traditional ways of healing in different cultures. We'll start with Native Americans in the United States. As you may know, the Native Americans have many ways of healing people. The Navajo people, in the southwestern part of the United States, are one good example. They use sand paintings to **heal** someone. So today I want to talk about how a sand painting is made and used. I would like to describe this process to you, and I think you'll find it very interesting, but first, let me give you a little background.

What are sand paintings, and who makes them? Let's start with who. . . . Who makes a sand painting? Well, a sand painting is made by a medicine man. The medicine man is a special person who studies for many years. The people of the **tribe trust** him very deeply and believe he can heal someone who is sick. They believe he heals by bringing the sick person back into **balance,** heals the sick person by, um, bringing the person back into balance with the world. And, one way he does this is by making a sand painting. It is made as part of a healing **ceremony.** OK, now here's how it's done.

When someone becomes seriously sick, the medicine man is called. He's called to visit the sick person. Now first, first, he must decide what the person's problem is. After he decides what the

problem is, he chooses the right healing **chant.** There are different chants for different **illnesses,** and these chants tell stories about Navajo **heroes.** OK, the chants tell stories about heroes. . . . These heroes go on **adventures** to reach the **gods** and get **cures** for human illnesses. These are stories that the Navajo people all know very well.

Now that's the first step—deciding the correct chant. After the medicine man decides on the correct chant, he is ready to make the sand painting. The sand painting and the chant that the medicine man uses are **related.** They are both about the same story. For example, look at the figure on page 44. This sand painting is called "Sun and Eagle." It is used with a healing chant for a sick child. The figure in the middle **represents** the child.

Now to start the sand painting, the medicine man first prepares a **bed** of white sand. Then he slowly creates the sand painting. He paints by letting the colors slowly **slide** down from his right hand. It looks simple to do, but it is very difficult to do well. The medicine man has to add many **details** to the sand painting. Each small thing added to the painting has a special meaning. He can't leave anything out. And he uses five main colors: white, black, blue, yellow, and red. Each color has a special meaning.

Narrator: Stop the tape and answer the questions for Part 1.

Narrator: Now let's continue with Part 2. In this part of the lecture, you will hear more about how sand paintings are used. You will also hear more about the meaning of sand paintings in the Navajo culture.

PART 2

When the medicine man finishes making the sand painting, the sick person is brought to it, brought to the sand painting. Next, the **patient** undresses and sits in the center of the sand painting, **facing** east. Then, the patient is "sung over." To be sung over means the medicine man has to do several things, including singing and chanting. The medicine man sings and chants, and as he sings, he **touches** a place on the painting and then touches the sick person. He continues to touch a place on the painting and then touch the sick person. He doesn't actually move the sand. What he does instead is **transfer** the healing energy of the sand painting onto the sick person. He carries this healing energy to the person. The Navajos believe this healing energy will get rid of the problem. It will remove the reason the person is out of balance—help to bring the person back into balance. This is the only way the person can become healthy again.

After the ceremony, the sand painting is **destroyed.** The sand is put on to a special blanket and taken outside. Then, the medicine man walks around and throws the sand. He throws it to carry away the sickness.

The Navajo people consider a sand painting very **holy,** very **powerful.** They believe that it must be made, used, and destroyed all within twelve hours. It can't be kept longer than this, no longer than twelve hours. This means that a sand painting made during the day must be destroyed by **sunset.** A sand painting made during the night must be destroyed before **sunrise** the next day. If a healing ceremony lasts more than one day, a different sand painting must be made each day.

Now, before I forget, let me go back and talk about the five main colors that are used. As I said earlier, the five colors are white, black, blue, yellow, and red. Each color has its own special meaning. Each color, except for red, is the **symbol** of a **season** of the year and a direction. White stands for spring and east. It's a symbol of **dawn,** of new beginnings. Then comes yellow. Yellow means autumn and west. It represents sunset, getting older. Then comes blue. Blue is a symbol of south and summer. It stands for **middle age** and happiness. Next is black. Black represents winter and north. Black stands for night, old age, death. Finally, there is red. Red represents **power** and danger.

The Navajo people believe that the world we live in is in a very **delicate** balance. Everything has its place. Only people can **disturb** the balance. Illness is a sign that the balance has been **upset.** By chanting and making the sand painting, the medicine man works to bring balance back. This is the only way the sick person can get well.

OK, so those are some of the ideas behind sand paintings and the process for using them. Next class, we'll talk about other cultures and ways of healing.

Narrator: Stop the tape and answer the questions for Part 2.

UNIT 7 Sound

Narrator: In this first part of the lecture, you are going to hear about sound waves. Look at the figures in your book as you listen.

PART 1

Today I am going to talk about something very basic in our lives—sound. As you know, sound is all around us. Every day we hear hundreds of sounds. Think for a minute. Try to remember three sounds you heard today. OK, now write them down . . . . Probably you can remember a lot of sounds you have heard today.

Have you ever asked yourself, What is a sound? Actually, a sound is simply a **series** of **air pressure** changes. We can make a sound by speaking, by dropping a book, or by hitting a baseball. However the sound is made, in each case we are changing the air pressure.

Look at the figure on page 52. Follow closely as I explain what happens when a sound is made. In the figure, you see a **tuning fork** with circles around it. Notice the labels *a* and *b*. These are the **prongs** of the tuning fork. The circles are the **areas** of air pressure of a sound wave. A sound wave has three areas: one of high air pressure, one of low air pressure, and one of **neutral** pressure. Again, one high, one low, and one neutral. The area of high pressure is called a *compression,* c-o-m-p-r-e-s-s-i-o-n. The area of low pressure is called a *rarefaction,* r-a-r-e-f-a-c-t-i-o-n. The area of neutral pressure has the same air pressure as before the tuning fork is struck.

When you **strike** a tuning fork, the prongs **vibrate.** They move back and forth in the air around the tuning fork. This makes a series of compressions and rarefactions. In a compression, the **molecules** of air are crowded together. This makes them push against the next layer of air, and the wave of compression **spreads out.** In a rarefaction, the molecules spread apart—they become very thin. Other molecules move in to fill the empty space. As these molecules move in, this **creates** another empty space, another rarefaction. So, do you see what I mean? We can say that sound is created by the molecules of air pushing together and **thinning out.** The sound continues until the series of compressions and rarefactions stops.

All right, so the complete series of compressions and rarefactions is called a sound wave. Another way to say this is that a sound wave is a series of air pressure changes. Of course, these changes, the compressions and rarefactions, happen very quickly. To give you an example, a sound that is loud enough for us to hear must have a **rate** of 20 compressions and 20 rarefactions **per second.**

Narrator: Stop the tape and answer the questions for Part 1.

Narrator: Now let's continue with Part 2. In this part of the lecture, you will hear about two ways of recording, or storing, sound.

PART 2

OK, now that you understand how sound is made, I'd like to change the topic a bit. Now I'd like to talk about **recording** sound. There are two main ways that sounds are recorded. One way is called **analog.** That's a-n-a-l-o-g. The other way is called **digital**—d-i-g-i-t-a-l. For both ways of recording, for both analog and digital recording, a microphone is used. The changes in air pressure—in other words, the sound—acts on the microphone and makes an electrical signal. OK, got that? The main difference between analog and digital recording is how the sound is **stored.** Listen carefully now as I compare analog and digital recording.

Let me see. To understand analog recording, I guess you need to know what analog means. An analog is a picture or **representation** of something. In analog recording, the sound that comes through the microphone is **copied** as a picture of the **original** sound waves. This picture or representation is recorded onto **magnetic tape.** The magnetic **pattern** on the tape is an analog, in other words, a kind of picture, of the original sound. The sound is stored as a **continuous** stream of magnetism. Another way to think of this is that the shape of the magnetism on the tape looks like a picture of the sound. This is shown in the top figure on page 53.

In a digital recording, the sound is stored differently. It isn't a picture or direct representation of the sound. It is stored electronically as small **bits of information.** These bits of information are in the form of off–on **binary codes,** off or on binary codes. These are represented in the figure as ones and zeros.

When the digital recording is **played back,** the small bits of information are put back together so that we hear a continuous sound, in other words, a **melody,** a song, or whatever. The sound, however, is not stored as a continuous stream. It is stored as bits of information. This is the main difference between digital and analog recording.

As you probably know, digital recording is becoming more and more **popular.** Many people feel that digital recordings sound better. How about you—which do you prefer?

Narrator: Stop the tape and answer the questions for Part 2.

UNIT 8 Deserts: They Keep Expanding

Narrator: In this lecture, you will learn about the spread of deserts throughout the world. As you listen, think about the reasons deserts are spreading.

PART 1

Hello class. Let's begin. Today I am going to talk about desert areas. It's important for us to learn why desert areas are **increasing** all over the world. There are three main reasons for this, and I'm going to talk about these three main reasons, the reasons why the amount of **productive** land is **decreasing** all over the world.

OK, first, let's look at what a desert is. This will help us understand why desert **regions** are **spreading.** Simply, a desert is a very dry region. It usually has only a few plants and animals and it doesn't really have enough **moisture** for many plants or animals to live. It is not productive land.

Look at the figure on page 57—see the deserts? You see that the largest desert regions are near the **equator.** However, there are other large areas in the world that are becoming very dry.

Why is this? Why are they becoming dry? These areas have less rain now than they used to have. There are fewer plants, too. With fewer plants, it is more difficult for the **ground** to hold moisture. And, the moisture **evaporates** more quickly. As a result, new deserts are **appearing.**

People have given different reasons why these dry, unproductive areas are increasing. Some people like to say it's because of the weather. They say it is just the way nature is. Nature simply tends to produce dry regions.

But, wait a second. Let's think about this. Is nature really the problem? According to a large group of scientists, weather isn't the main problem; people are the main problem. When they say people are the problem, they mean people's actions—how people use and **manage** good, **fertile** land. If people don't **take care of** the land, it gets **destroyed.** The **topsoil,** which is the top, rich layer of **soil,** in many parts of the world is **eroding** rapidly. It's getting worn out. The result is that less and less good land is **available** for raising food or animals.

Narrator: Stop the tape and answer the questions for Part 1.

Narrator: Now let's continue with Part 2. Why are deserts expanding? In this part of the lecture, you will hear three reasons.

PART 2

OK, let's review for a second. When we say that people are the problem in the increase of deserts, we mean that people are **mismanaging** the land; they are not managing it well, not managing it correctly. We have identified some of the reasons why topsoil is eroding, why it is disappearing so quickly. Look at the figure on page 61 for a moment. As you can see, scientists have come up with three main causes: The first is overgrazing of farm animals, the second is overcutting of trees, and the third is poor methods of farming. Overgrazing, overcutting, and poor farming methods. Let's look at these one at a time.

In the figure you can see that 35 percent of topsoil is lost or destroyed because of farm animals overgrazing. Overgrazing means the animals eat away too many of the plants, too much of the plant growth as they **graze.** There are two results of overgrazing: First, when the animals, the cattle or sheep, for example, eat away the plants, there aren't enough plants left to hold the soil. If there aren't enough plants, the topsoil washes away. OK? That's very clear; the topsoil washes away without enough plants to hold it. Second, as the animals walk

around, they **pack down** the soil. As a result, the land can't hold moisture as well as it could before. The land gets drier, and fewer plants can grow.

Next, notice that 30 percent of the loss of good land is because of . . . well, it's due to overcutting of trees. Too many trees are cut and not replanted. They are cut down to use for fuel for cooking and heating. And, they are cut down to make room for factories or for farming. These are common reasons for overcutting. But, of course, if trees are not replanted, there is nothing to hold the soil. The wind and water carry it away—in other words, it erodes.

Next, notice that 28 percent is because of poor methods of farming. For example, farmers may use too much **fertilizer.** Or they don't let the land rest from year to year. Another big problem is that poor **irrigation** allows too much salt to build up in the soil. Then the soil isn't able to produce **crops** at all. All of these are poor methods of farming.

OK, so those are the causes. Now let's think about what this means for us. This loss of productive land is a **worldwide** problem. According to one organization, called EarthSave, 52 million acres of good land in the world become unproductive every year. That's 52 million acres every year! Some places are worse than others, such as parts of Africa, Asia, and South America. There, the problem is especially bad. However, farmland in places like the United States is eroding, too. According to the United States Department of Agriculture, 5 billion tons of topsoil are lost every year on **agricultural** land in the United States.

The lesson for us is obvious. People all over the world need to take better care of the soil. They need to change how they farm. The need to replant trees. Otherwise, there will be less and less productive land to feed more and more people.

Narrator: Stop the tape and answer the questions for Part 2.

UNIT 9 Photographs Today: Do They Tell the Truth?

Narrator: In this lecture, you will hear about techniques of changing photographs. In the first part, you will learn about electronic imaging.

PART 1

Today we're going to be talking about photojournalism, and especially I want to touch on some of the **ethical** questions photojournalists **face** . . . problems that they face because of the **technology available** to them in their work. Now photojournalists have a very important job in reporting the news. When I think of a photojournalist, I think of someone whose job it is to take pictures of **events** as they happen. This may mean pictures of wars, of storms, of presidents meeting people, or of football games and **parades.** The pictures give us information about what is going on in our world.

Nowadays, photojournalists have a variety of equipment available to them, not just their cameras. Today I want to focus on their use of computers, how photojournalists might use computers. The first point is this: With computers it is very easy for photographers to change the pictures they take. They can change the content, what's in the picture. They can do this to get just the picture they want.

One technique they can use is called electronic imaging. Not long ago, in fact only five or ten years ago, electronic imaging could only be done by people who had special **training.** Now, anyone can do it, anyone who has the right computer system. With electronic imaging, a photograph or an image is put into a computer. When it is in the computer, it can be changed in **basic** ways, and it is very difficult to tell that the photograph has been changed. For example, let's say a photographer took a picture of the **prime minister** of England, the president of the United States, and the prime minister of Japan at a meeting. With electronic imaging, the photographer could move the three people closer together or farther apart, or take one of them out of the picture completely, or even make them smile more. Or the photographer could even change their smiles to **frowns** to make people believe something went wrong at the meeting. Isn't that amazing to think about?

It's important to point out that changing photographs isn't new. In the past, however, it was easy to tell that a photo had been changed. This was especially true with color photography. Now, however, it is much easier to change what's in a photograph. It is also much harder, or even impossible, to tell that the photograph has been changed. This is the problem we have to consider.

Narrator: Stop the tape and answer the questions for Part 1.

Narrator: Now let's continue with Part 2. In this part of the lecture, the speaker will discuss the question: Is it right for photographers and photojournalists to use electronic imaging? Think about this question as you listen.

PART 2

Now let's look at a basic question: Is there anything wrong with **altering** photographs? For a long, long time people have believed that photographs tell us the **truth;** they tell us what *really* happened. There are some common expressions based on this belief. One of them is "Photographs don't **lie.**" If you tell me you didn't go to a party, but I have a picture of you at the party, what is the truth—your word or the photo? Most people would say that the photograph tells the true story.

Another expression is "One picture is **worth** a thousand words." . . . "One picture is worth a thousand words." This means a picture says more than words. These expressions are **based on** the idea that a photograph is more **believable,** more "true," more complete than words can ever be.

In recent times, however, the situation is very different. Now, photographs can be changed by electronic imaging. In the past, photographs could be used as **proof.** I could say, "I know you were at the party. I have a picture to **prove** it." Now, however, you could tell me that a computer put you into the photograph. In other words, the photograph I have isn't really true or believable.

OK, so let's return to our basic question: What effect will electronic imaging have on photojournalism? This is a question that the **media,** in general, is facing now. The **rules** are slowly being made as the use of electronic imaging spreads. When electronic imaging was first being used, the magazine ***National Geographic*** got into trouble. Here's what happened. In 1982, a photographer decided to move two Egyptian **pyramids** closer together so that they would fit on the cover of the magazine. OK, the photographer altered the picture by cutting some space between the two giant pyramids. Many people noticed this and felt it wasn't right. They asked, "Is it all right for a photographer to change facts in this way?"

Then, in 1987, there was a similar situation. *Time magazine* took a photograph of some people inside a **studio,** and they used this photograph in an important story. But they used it in the story so that it looked like the photograph had been taken at the **American Embassy** in Moscow. Again people said, "No, that's not all right." Since then, there have been many, many examples of photographs of sporting events, politicians, and movie stars that have been altered.

Today, there are no firm rules that all newspapers and magazines must follow. Some magazines **admit** that they alter photographs. Some say they will change a photograph to make someone look better, but not to change who is in the picture. Other magazines and newspapers say they never alter their photographs. Never.

So let's summarize the ethical problem here. Photographers have the technology available to them to alter their photographs in many ways. What is the **responsibility** of photojournalists? What if a photographer decided to change a war photo or an accident photo to make it "worse"? Or, what if a photographer removes some people from a photograph to make a street look less crowded? Some photographers might say, "Why not? With modern technology, it's just so easy to **manipulate** images and objects for the effect you want." Well, what do *you* think?

In my opinion, we have to think seriously about the uses of electronic imaging. We have to ask ourselves some serious questions about how and when it is used. I personally think electronic imaging can be dangerous. People still need to believe that photographs don't lie.

Narrator: Stop the tape and answer the questions for Part 2.

UNIT 10 Allergies

Narrator: In this part of the lecture, you will learn about allergic reactions. What happens when a person has an allergic reaction? Think about this question as you listen.

PART 1

Today I think we are ready to start talking about allergies . . . and about allergic reactions. In the first part of my lecture, I'm going to explain what an allergic reaction is. Then I will try to describe what an allergic reaction to a **bee sting** is like. In the second part of my lecture, I'm going to talk about allergy testing and allergy shots. I'll explain one way the testing is done. I'll also tell you how and why allergy shots are given. That's a lot to cover, so let's begin.

What is an allergic reaction? Well, an allergic reaction is really an action of the **immune system** in the body, an action of the immune system in your body. The immune system's job is to protect you, to make **antibodies** to protect you from things that are dangerous to your health. In an allergic reaction, however, your body makes antibodies to something that isn't really a problem for the body—that is, it's not usually a problem for someone without an allergy. For example, milk and cat hair and dust are usually not dangerous to humans. But, for some reason, your body might produce antibodies to milk or to cat hair or to dust. Your body is trying to protect you from these things.

When the immune system does this, it is, in a sense, working too hard. The result is a fight. The fight is between your antibodies and the milk you drank or the cat hair or the dust you breathed in. You know your body is having a fight because you **sneeze,** or you have red, **itchy** eyes and a **runny nose,** or you feel tired, or you may have **difficulty breathing.** These are some of the common signs of an allergy.

Now let's turn our attention to one specific allergic reaction. Let's look at what happens with a bee sting. Anyone who gets a bee sting will have some reaction. A normal reaction is **pain** and **swelling** and redness where the sting is. This type of reaction is also called a local reaction because the reaction is only in the location, the place, where the sting is.

In contrast, an allergic reaction to a bee sting is a much stronger reaction. It is a general reaction that affects the whole body. This general reaction is called an anaphylactic reaction, a-n-a-p-h-y-l-a-c-t-i-c. This is shown in the figure on page 76, so take a look at the figure. In this kind of reaction, several things happen. There is pain and swelling, but it is *all over* the body, not just where the sting is. The person's legs, arms, feet, and face usually itch and turn red. It often becomes difficult for the person to breathe. The person can also become weak and **confused.** The **blood pressure** may drop. For some people, these reactions may continue for hours unless some medicine is given. In fact, the person can die if he or she isn't given medicine to stop the reaction.

Narrator: Stop the tape and answer the questions for Part 1.

Narrator: Now let's continue with Part 2. In this part of the lecture, the speaker will explain one approach to treating allergic reactions. What is this approach? How does it work?

PART 2

Now, if you are allergic to something, it's important to know how to prevent these reactions. One question is, How do people know if they are allergic to something, say, if they are allergic to bee stings? One way to find out is to have an allergy test. One type of test is a skin test. To do the test, the doctor **injects** a small amount of the **venom,** the **poison** from the bee, under the skin. You can see this in the left hand figure on page 77. Then, the doctor watches closely to see what happens. The doctor pays attention to two things: the color of the skin and the size of the **bump** on the skin. This is shown in the right hand figure on the same page. If the skin reacts strongly—in other words, if the bump is big and very red—this means the person is very allergic. If the skin only changes a little, the person is only **slightly** allergic. If the skin doesn't change, this usually means the person isn't allergic.

If the doctor finds out the person is allergic to bees, or bee stings, allergy shots are often recommended. In the allergy shots, the doctor uses a small amount of bee venom. The doctor does this to make the person less **sensitive** to the venom; in other words, to build up the person's **immunity** to the venom. This is similar to what doctors do when they give children shots against **childhood diseases** like **measles.**

Each visit, the doctor increases the amount of venom in the shot. The doctor starts off with a very small amount of venom and uses slightly more each time. Increasing the amount builds up immunity to the venom. This immunity will not protect the person from a bee sting, of course. If the person gets stung, he or she will still get a local reaction, but will not have an allergic reaction. OK, so that's basically how the allergy shots work.

To sum up the main points of our talk today, let's recall what an allergic reaction is and how allergic reactions can be prevented. Remember that an allergic reaction is an unusual reaction to something that doesn't normally affect people. In an allergic reaction, for example, to a bee sting, the body keeps producing antibodies and the person can have an anaphylactic reaction. This can be very serious, and the person may even die if he or she isn't given medicine. Allergy shots help to prevent an allergic reaction. They help make someone less sensitive to the thing that causes the allergy, such as the bee venom.

OK, well, if you can remember these points, I think that's all for today.

Narrator: Stop the tape and answer the questions for Part 2.

UNIT 11 World Music

Narrator: In this part of the lecture on music, you will hear the speaker's ideas about modern music.

PART 1

OK, everybody, let's begin. Today's topic is music, world music. We'll be talking about music from all over the world. Now just think for a minute, think about the great variety of music that is available to us . . . just a fantastic variety. And today I want to focus, in particular, on the **transmission,** or spread, of music . . . how music spreads all over the world.

Nowadays, it's very easy for people to hear music from other cultures. Of course, it's recordings, recorded music, that makes this possible. In old times, long before recorded music, the transmission and variety of music people heard was **limited** by two things: people's **memory** and how far they could travel. If people had good memories, they could remember the songs they heard, and play them later themselves. If they could walk to the next **village,** they could learn the music played there.

That was the beginning of the spread of music. But, in modern times, nowadays, obviously the situation is very different. Recorded music is everywhere. Music seems to be everywhere we go. We now expect to hear music in restaurants, doctor's offices, airports, and so on. In addition, compact disk (CD) players, tape recorders, radios, and other types of equipment aren't expensive. They are **affordable** to many people. As a result, most people have some way of listening to recorded music at home.

Now, we probably all think that this is a positive thing. But there are some **negative** effects of music being so easily available. For one thing, many people have become **passive** listeners to music. By this I mean music is something that is just there; people don't really listen to it. In addition, fewer and fewer people play musical instruments for fun. There just aren't many **amateur** musicians. People **rely on** the professionals to make the music instead. Think for a minute about your own country and your own family. Who plays music? At what age do people study music? How many adults do you know who play musical instruments? When do they play them?

Narrator: Stop the tape and answer the questions for Part 1.

Narrator: Now let's continue with Part 2. In this part of the lecture, the speaker explains the effects of the rapid spread of music and musical styles. You will hear several examples in this part of the lecture.

PART 2

OK, well let's continue. Even though recorded music seems to have had some negative effects, it has also had some very positive effects. One of these is . . . it has had a great effect on **enriching** the variety of music we hear. Recording has given us **access,** access to music we just wouldn't know otherwise. Nowadays, it is very easy for people to hear music from different cultures. For example, a Japanese student can buy recordings of **American** **bluegrass** or **Balinese classical** music. A teenager in New York or Paris can buy **popular Arabic** music. An Italian rock group can buy and hear **Caribbean** and **African** music. There are probably other examples you can think of.

This spread, this transmission, of musical styles throughout the world is **accelerating,** it's growing. As a result, a type of music called World Music is developing. World Music—have you heard that term before? World Music is an international style of music that combines African music, **reggae** from the Caribbean, European instruments, and other types of regional music. It uses **traditional** and modern music together in **unique** ways that are very exciting. Well, I think it's very exciting . . . . For example, many African musicians have combined traditional African music with European and electronic instruments in very creative ways. Sunny Ade from Nigeria and Manu Dibango from Cameroon are two of my favorites, and they are just two of the many African musicians who have done this.

I'd like to give you a few more examples of some of the World Music that is being created. Paul Simon—most of you must know him—Paul Simon's music of the late 80s and early 90s is a good example. His famous album, *Graceland,* was on the **pop charts** for two years, and sold over 8 million copies. Wow! That means a lot of people are buying recordings of World Music. To make *Graceland,* Paul Simon traveled to South Africa where he met with **local** musicians. They combined traditional African sounds with his music to create something new. *Graceland* made many people more aware of African music. The South African group, Ladysmith Black Mambazo, that recorded with Paul Simon later made a successful album of their own without him. Paul Simon's next album, *Rhythm of the Saints,* is another example. To make it, he went to Brazil four times. Again, he played with the local musicians and created something new, something unique, something the world had never heard before.

There are many, many other examples—exciting, creative examples—but I'll just mention one more. This is another favorite of mine. It's an album called *A World Out Of Time.* This album was made in 1991 by two Americans, Henry Kaiser and David Lindley. They went to Madagascar. Have any of you ever been there, to Madagascar? No? Well, in Madagascar, they met some local musicians who they played music with all day, every day, for two weeks. They recorded enough music to make five CDs. Some of the music is the local music, some is their own music, and some is a new style of music they created together with the local musicians. This music is now available in record stores for anyone to buy.

Many examples like this can be found throughout the world, and new examples are being created now, right as we speak. Some people have said that this accelerated spread of music is a bad thing. They feel it will weaken the traditional music of each country, and eventually music everywhere will sound the same. There is another way of thinking about what is happening now: namely, that it is very exciting. Recording makes it possible for musicians to create new types of music and for us to have a wide variety of musical experiences.

Narrator: Stop the tape and answer the questions for Part 2.

UNIT 12 Preventing Disasters

Narrator: In the first part of the lecture, you will learn the difference between a natural hazard and a natural disaster. The speaker will give one example of a natural disaster that occurred in South America.

PART 1

Today I want to talk with you about natural **hazards**—hurricanes, volcanic eruptions, and so on. Of course, we can't stop them, but we can prepare for them. So today, I'll focus on how we can try to prepare for natural hazards. Preparing means, well, it means planning ahead, and planning isn't easy. Good planning takes scientific information, it takes money, and it takes **cooperation** between scientists and governments.

In this lecture, I'm first going to give you a little bit of background, background information. Then I'm going to talk specifically about one incident, a volcano that **erupted** in Colombia, South America. And then, finally, I'm going to give you some ideas about planning, a general **plan** for preparing for a natural hazard.

Nowadays, many of us are concerned about what we are doing *to* the environment. We worry about what is happening to the air, the water, and the land. But we also need to think about what the environment can do *to us.* There are many things that happen in **nature** that can be dangerous to us. For example, there are **hurricanes,** earthquakes, **droughts, wildfires, floods,** and volcanic eruptions. These are all examples of natural hazards.

Any of these natural hazards can become a natural **disaster.** A natural disaster means the earthquake or the hurricane does terrible things to people. People are killed or hurt, or their houses are **damaged** or **destroyed,** or their businesses and **property** are lost. There is a lot of **destruction.** It takes a lot of time and money and energy for **communities** to **recover** and return to normal life.

Now, let's remember that there is nothing we can do to stop natural hazards. They have always happened, and they always will happen. We can, however, **control,** or, um, control to some extent, whether a natural hazard becomes a disaster or not. The key is planning.

Any country or any city needs to have a plan based on understanding what natural hazards occur there. By understanding the hazards, people can plan ways to have fewer problems if a natural hazard occurs. But making a plan is very **complicated** because there are many things to think about, things to consider. Now before I talk about planning, let me tell you about one situation. This was a volcanic eruption that occurred in Colombia in 1985. After you understand this situation, we can use it as an example for planning.

OK, here we are. November 1985, Colombia. The volcano Nevado del Ruiz erupts. For one year before the eruption, the volcano had been making noises. There were signs something was going on. Then, there was a small eruption. The eruption wasn't so big, but it melted snow and ice at the top of the volcano. The water moved down the sides of the volcano and joined with water in the ground, and this caused **mudflows.** An example of a mudflow is shown in the figure on page 92.

In this case, the mudflows quickly **swept** through several towns. More than 25,000 people were killed . . . 25,000 people killed. And scientists had been watching the volcano and *knew* early that there was danger. Unfortunately, the people weren't prepared.

A disaster resulted: Towns were destroyed and, as I said, 25,000 people were killed.

Narrator: Stop the tape and answer the questions for Part 1.

Narrator: now let's continue with Part 2. In this part, the speaker will explain the idea of planning to prevent disasters and planning to respond to emergencies that happen.

PART 2

OK, now this was a major disaster. Is there any lesson for us here? The big lesson from Nevado del Ruiz is that it is important to plan and prepare. Well, that's easy for us to say! Of course, this is not easy to do. Governments often have to choose, to decide between taking care of real problems they have now and planning for problems they *might* have in the future. A country or city needs to have a basic plan, though.

The plan should include three **phases:** what to do before, during, and after a disaster occurs. OK, three phases to a plan, a "before" phase, a "during" phase, and an "after" phrase—oh, excuse me, not *phrase,* but *phase*—an "after" phase.

The "before" phase consists of learning about the problem—gathering information, both general and specific information. In the case of volcanoes, scientists need to have a general understanding of volcanoes all over the world. They need to study what volcanoes have done in the past and what volcanoes, in general, are like.

At the same time, they need to gather information about a particular place. To use Nevado del Ruiz as an example, scientists must study what the volcanic activity is there. They need to study what has happened in Colombia in the past and what is happening now. Then they can use this specific information to say what might happen in Colombia in the future. They need to study this information very carefully.

Another part of the "before" phase is studying land use. The government needs to get information from scientists about what parts of the country or city might be dangerous. Then the government can think about controlling where people live and work.

I'll emphasize here that the government can *think* about controlling where people can live and work, or I guess they can *try* to control where people can live and work. Of course, it is very difficult to *tell* people where they can or cannot live and work, but doing this can possibly save money and lives.

In Colombia, scientists made **maps** of the area around Nevado del Ruiz. They marked on the maps the areas that appeared the most dangerous to live and work in. They gave these maps to the government. Unfortunately, the government wasn't able to use the information before the volcano erupted. Many people were living in these dangerous areas.

OK, well, let's move on. The second phase is the "during" phase. This phase includes what to do *if* a natural hazard occurs. This, in other words, is an **emergency** plan. The government needs to make a plan so that everyone knows what to do if something happens. People must know where to go, how to get there, and which **routes** to take. They need to know where water, medicine, and food will be. The plan must include how the people and the police and fire departments will all work together. According to scientists, the number of people who died from Nevado del Ruiz could have been a lot fewer if there had been a good emergency plan.

Finally, there is the "after" phrase, I mean the "after" phase. This is the recovery after a disaster. The government needs to plan how people will return to a normal life after the damage is done. The plan should include who will do the work, when it will be done, and who will pay for it.

As I have been saying today, making a good general plan is not easy. It's not as easy as it looks. It takes money, scientific information, and, most of all, good cooperation between scientists and governments. Many countries all over the world are working on this now.

OK, so this is just a brief look at a very complicated problem. How can governments control whether a natural hazard becomes a disaster? Next time, we'll look at what some countries are doing to deal with the problem. OK, great, let's stop here for today.

Narrator: Stop the tape and answer the questions for Part 2.

CREDITS

Alter, Jonathan. "When Photographs Lie." *Newsweek,* 30 July 1990, 44–45.

Berland, Theodore, and Lucia Fischer-Pap. *Living with Your Allergies and Asthma.* New York: St. Martin's Press, 1983.

Decker, Robert and Barbara. "Reducing Volcanic Risk." *Earthquakes and Volcanoes* 22, no. 3 (1991): 129–130.

Filson, Brent. *There's a Monster in Your Closet.* New York: Simon and Schuster, Julian Messner Publisher, 1986.

Gigliesi, Primerose, and Robert C. Friend, trans. *The Effendi and the Pregnant Pot: Uygur Folktales from China.* Beijing: New World Press, 1982.

Glidden, Judith. "Cattlemen's Group: Opponents Skew the Facts." *Minuteman Chronicle,* 7 Nov. 1992, 1, 8.

Hall, Minard L. "Advances (?) in Mitigating Volcanic Hazards in Latin America." *Earthquakes and Volcanoes* 22, no. 3 (1991): 149–150.

Harris, Phillip R., and Robert T. Morgan. *Managing Cultural Differences.* Houston: Gulf Publishing Co., 1979.

Jones, Rhoda Dankin. "Word Muddles: New Theories about Dyslexia." *American Health,* Sept. 1992, 65–69.

Kaiser, Henry, and David Lindley. *A World Out of Time.* Shanachie Records, 1991.

Levinson, Harold N., and Addie Sanders. *The Upside-Down Kids.* New York: M. Evans and Co., Inc., 1991.

Macaulay, David. *The Way Things Work.* Boston: Houghton Mifflin, 1988.

McCrum, Robert, William Cran, and Robert MacNeil. *The Story of English.* New York: Viking Penguin, Elisabeth Sifton Books, 1986.

MILES Pharmaceutical Division. "Venom Attack Force." Patient information. U.S.A.: MILES, 1988.

The New Book of Popular Science. Vol. 3, *Physical Sciences.* Danbury, Conn.: Grolier International, 1990.

Scheele, Adele. "Are You a Bad Boss?" *Working Woman,* April 1992, 32–33.

Stevens, Laura J. *The Complete Book of Allergy Control.* New York: Macmillan, 1983.

Strahler, Arthur N. *Principles of Earth Science.* New York: Harper and Row, 1976.

Stroh, M., and J. Raloff. "New UN Soil Survey: The Dirt on Erosion." *Science News,* 4 April 1992, 215.

Task Group for International Decade of Disaster Reduction. "Reducing Volcanic Disasters in the 1990s." Draft. July 1989.

Tilling, Robert I. "Coping with Volcanic Hazards: A Global Perspective." *Earthquakes and Volcanoes* 22, no. 4 (1990): 154–160.